Rethinking Global Governance

Rethinking Global Governance

Thomas G. Weiss and Rorden Wilkinson

polity

First published in 2019 by Polity Press

Reprinted 2020

Polity Press
65 Bridge Street
Cambridge CB2 1UR, UK

Polity Press
101 Station Landing
Suite 300
Medford, MA 02155, USA

ISBN-13: 978-1-5095-2723-6
ISBN-13: 978-1-5095-2724-3 (pb)

A catalogue record for this book is available from the British Library.

Typeset in 10 on 16.5pt Utopia by
Servis Filmsetting Ltd, Stockport, Cheshire
Printed and bound in the United States by LSC Communications

For further information on Polity, visit our website:
politybooks.com

Contents

About the Authors

Thomas G. Weiss is fighting valiantly against senior moments and creaking joints as Presidential Professor of Political Science at the Graduate Center of the City University of New York and Director Emeritus of the Ralph Bunche Institute for International Studies; he is also Eminent Scholar at Kyung Hee University, Korea. He was a 2016 Andrew Carnegie Fellow and a past president of the International Studies Association (2009-10) as well as the recipient of its "2016 Distinguished IO Scholar Award." Other previous posts were as Research Professor at SOAS, University of London (2012-15), Chair of the Academic Council on the UN System (2006-9), editor of Global Governance (2000-5), and Research Director of the International Commission on Intervention and State Sovereignty (2000-1). He has written extensively about multilateral approaches to international peace and security, humanitarian action, and sustainable development, and his latest single-authored books are *Would the World Be Better without the UN?* (2018); *What's Wrong with the United Nations and How to Fix It* (2016); *Humanitarian Intervention: Ideas in Action* (2016); *Governing the World? Addressing "Problems without Passports"* (2014); *Global Governance: Why? What? Whither?* (2013); *Humanitarian Business* (2013); and *Thinking about Global Governance: People and Ideas Matter* (2011).

Rorden Wilkinson is Deputy Pro-Vice-Chancellor for Education and Innovation, Professor of Global Political Economy, and a Fellow of the UK Trade Policy Observatory at the University of Sussex. He has held visiting positions at the Australian National University, Brown University, and Wellesley College, and an honorary professorial post at the University of Manchester, where he was previously Professor of International Political Economy and Research Director of the Brooks World Poverty Institute. In 2017–18 he was Vice-President of the International Studies Association (ISA). He is a member of the editorial board of the international public policy journal *Global Governance*, a Fellow of the Royal Society of Arts, and the 2014 recipient of the ISA Society for Women in International Political Economy (SWIPE) Mentoring Award. He has written extensively on global governance, trade, development, and global public policy. His most recent books include *What's the Point of International Relations?* (2017); *What's Wrong with the WTO and How to Fix It* (2014); *Trade, Poverty, Development: Getting beyond the WTO's Doha Deadlock* (2013); *The Millennium Development Goals and Beyond: Global Development after 2015* (2012); and *Global Governance, Poverty, and Inequality* (2010).

Together, Weiss and Wilkinson edit the "Global Institutions" series for Routledge and are co-editors of *International Organization and Global Governance* (2nd edn, 2018).

Preface

After we assembled the final proposal for this volume in early 2017, we ran the term "global governance" though a Google search. We had done so previously and anticipated that the number of hits would be significant. Neither of us was quite ready for the 19 million that came back – 10 million more than when we edited a special section of a journal only two years earlier, and quite an astonishing number given that a quarter of a century ago the term was almost unknown. Our astonishment notwithstanding, what the results illustrated was that, for all its ubiquity, a settled understanding of global governance remains elusive. A cursory glance reveals that it is deployed in a wide variety of ways, including as an alternative moniker for international organizations; a descriptor for a global stage packed with ever more actors; a call to arms for a better world; an attempt to control the pernicious aspects of accelerating economic and social change; a synonym for world government; and a term for a perceived hegemonic plot to advance the interests of a murky global elite.

For two authors who have long worked at the coalface of what it is that we imagine global governance to be, the continuing combination of ubiquity and imprecision is a source of frustration and professional embarrassment. *Rethinking Global Governance* is our attempt to improve understanding in the field. It develops our 2014 *International Studies Quarterly* article exploring complexity, authority, power, and change in global governance and the discussion that it generated.[1] It extends the value that we identified in setting out the markers of a more analytically nourishing approach to global governance for the broader study of international relations (IR) that appeared in the journal *Global Governance* in 2014.[2] It moves forward our work on what drives change and continuity in a 2015 *Ethics & International Affairs* article, which appeared in a special issue that we edited.[3] It moves beyond a specifically commissioned chapter that appeared in the 2016 second edition of Ken Booth and Toni Erskine's *International Relations Theory Today*, which sought to probe the capacity of global governance to make sense of changed global circumstances.[4] It advances our commitment to recapturing the normative potential of global governance that appeared in a 2015 collection entitled *Rising Powers, Global Governance and Global Ethics*, edited by Jamie Gaskarth.[5] It extends our effort to consider the "everyday" experiences of the globally governed, which appeared in a 2018 issue of the journal *Global Governance*.[6] And it evolves organically from and builds creatively upon our long-standing individual and joint work addressing questions of global governance and world order, including the 2018 second edition of our 55-chapter textbook *International Organization and Global Governance*.[7] That said, while many of those thoughts make an appearance here, they form part of a deeper, more sustained engagement with the problematic of global governance and the journey toward its resolution that unfolds in the pages that follow.

We wanted to develop and take forward our own struggles not only because global governance remains without conceptual and analytical rigor but also because we see its normative potential ailing as a result. We were also motivated by a frustration at the tendency for scholars to fall back on the hardy perennials of IR theory for explanatory sustenance when thinking about global governance rather than developing custom-made analytical lenses or tailored theoretical frameworks.[8] While we see great value in knowing how global governance is explained through realist, feminist, constructivist, liberal institutionalist, Marxist, post-structural, and post- and de-colonial lenses, such diversity often tells us more about myriad theoretical flowers blooming than about global governance as a phenomenon. Because as a scholarly community we have been unable to arrive at a consensus on what global governance is, we are even less likely to be able to agree – as Klaus Dingworth and Philipp Pattberg remind us – on conclusions. Their worry, and one that we have also, is that our lack of shared understanding becomes even more problematic because persistent divisions inhibit an accumulation of insights that build upon one another and advance genuine comprehension.[9]

The result is that we have ceased to expand the boundaries of our understanding and have left unrealized the prescriptive potential that global governance could generate to provide better answers to genuine puzzles about world order as well as solutions to real-world problems. Indeed, the best that we can muster is that global governance is a catch-all label designed to indicate the highest level of analysis.[10] It is seldom applied to generate incisive understandings of how the world is ordered and governed or how it could be reorganized to bring about progressive change world-wide. It is little wonder that we are hardly further advanced in answering the question that Lawrence Finkelstein provocatively posed almost twenty-five years ago – "What is global governance?" His answer was "Virtually anything."[11]

Rethinking Global Governance seeks to attenuate confusion by reclaiming the term's unrealized analytical value and rescuing its normative potential. Our argument is that global governance must move from a simple association with the actions and activities of international organizations and their subsidiaries to a set of questions that probe the intricate and multifaceted manner in which the world is governed and ordered at a given moment in time. Only then will we find theoretically nourishing and empirically satisfying interpretations. We claim that these questions have the potential to generate better understandings of the complex elements that combine to produce distinctive world orders and that enable us to see how the world has been, is, and will be governed; account for the different systems of global governance that have existed across time and space as well as explore their peculiarities; comprehend the forces that have driven and continue to drive continuity and change in patterns of global governance and that propel stability and transformation, overlap, and ambiguity; and oblige us to examine the manner in which global governance is experienced by recipients through discovering what it is like to be on its receiving end.

Our purpose is not to advance a singular theory, because we are still asking first-order questions. Our own view is that we are at too early a stage in the process of refinement to attempt such an endeavor, though a recent laudable attempt has been made to do just that.[12] Instead, *Rethinking Global Governance* highlights the utility of continuing to ask questions and – just as crucially – of harnessing the normative potential of the answers for designing and helping implement better global governance. Ours is thus a plea for an urgent reconceptualization, which is stimulated by two distinct motivations: first, in an age of resurgent populism and nationalism – of which Trumpism and Brexit are two prominent illustrations – both the planet itself and the normative project of progressive global change are in peril;[13] and, second, as Craig Murphy aptly summarized, global governance remains "poorly done and poorly understood."[14]

We are grateful for thoughtful comments from three reviewers; the role of our fellow global governance scholars in sharpening our own thinking in numerous scholarly environs; the professionalism and good humor of Louise Knight, Nekane Tanaka Galdos, and the team at Polity Press; long car journeys, global airways, digital communication technologies, fine wine and craft beer; and the absences that our families have endured that made this volume possible. We would like to claim in particular that Priscilla Read and Claire Annesley have been patient in dealing with our obsession to get global governance right, or at least better. The mistakes, as always, are our own.

TGW and RW

New York and Brighton

July 2018

Abbreviations

ASEAN	Association of Southeast Asian Nations
AU	African Union
COMECON	Council for Mutual Economic Assistance
DfID	Department for International Development (UK)
EEC	European Economic Community
EU	European Union
FAO	Food and Agricultural Organization
FIFA	Fédération Internationale de Football Association
G77	Group of 77
GATT	General Agreement on Tariffs and Trade
ICANN	Internet Corporation for Assigned Names and Numbers
ICC	International Criminal Court
ICRC	International Committee of the Red Cross
IGO	intergovernmental organization
IL	international law
ILO	International Labour Organization

IMF	International Monetary Fund
IO	international organization
IOM	International Organization for Migration
IPE	international political economy
IPU	International Postal Union
IR	international relations
ITU	International Telecommunications Union
MDGs	Millennium Development Goals
MSF	Medécins Sans Frontières
MUNS	Multilateralism and the United Nations System
NAFTA	North American Free Trade Agreement
NAM	Non-Aligned Movement
NATO	North Atlantic Treaty Organization
NGO	non-governmental organization
OAS	Organization of American States
OAU	Organization of African Unity
OCHA	UN Office for the Coordination of Humanitarian Affairs
OECD	Organisation for Economic Co-operation and Development
SAARC	South Asian Association for Regional Cooperation
SDGs	Sustainable Development Goals
UK	United Kingdom
UN	United Nations
UNCTAD	UN Conference on Trade and Development
UNDP	UN Development Programme
UNESCO	UN Educational, Scientific and Cultural Organization
UNHCR	Office of the UN High Commissioner for Refugees
UNICEF	UN Children's Fund

UNO	United Nations Organization
UNRRA	UN Relief and Rehabilitation Administration
UNU	UN University
US	United States of America
WFP	World Food Programme
WHO	World Health Organization
WMD	weapons of mass destruction
WTO	World Trade Organization

Introduction: Back to Basics

Why should we care about global governance? What is it? What exactly is the point? Is it desirable? Can it make the world a better place? Almost three-quarters of a century after the end of World War II and the dropping of two atomic bombs – the first on Hiroshima, the second on Nagasaki – the record of global governance seems thin. Nuclear weapons once again threaten, this time on the other side of the Sea of Japan. Pernicious populism, nationalism, and far-right movements are on the rise in the United States, Europe, and elsewhere. Attempts to stem the rates of acceleration of global warming, desertification, and species extinction have faltered. Health pandemics threaten, anti-microbial resistance grows, and global prosperity stutters. Measured against the contemporary world, the system of global governance that emerged in 1945 appears unfit for purpose – and little better for successive attempts to reform its principal components.

Admittedly, today's global governance is not that of 1945, yet we persist in thinking as if it were. The post-war world order was crafted by the actions and activities of great powers; it reflects the peace settlement and institutional structures built by them. Elements remain, but today's order is also forged by financial markets, credit rating agencies, terrorist cells, civil wars, refugee flows, private military companies, global production networks, pirates, mega-corporations, and kids in bedrooms hacking government and commercial computer systems. It is no surprise that yesterday's global governance is ill-equipped to deal with the world order of today. However, this realization does not stop us from persisting with outmoded intellectual frameworks and old-fashioned policy responses. We remain enamored with global governance, nonetheless.

We are not the first to note, or even admire, such contradictions. In 1931 George Orwell, writing under his given name Eric Arthur Blair, published a review of Pearl S. Buck's *The Good Earth*. He began:

> This is a very exceptional book. It starts uncertainly, and it is handicapped by a bad style . . . But one scarcely worries about this, the story goes so straight to the very heart of truth. There is no plot, and yet not a single redundant incident; no words spent in pity, but a fidelity to life which simply withers optimism.[1]

Orwell was not alone in his assessment. *The Good Earth* won the 1932 Pulitzer Prize for Fiction. Strikingly, his summation of Buck's opus – foibles and all – could also describe the study of global governance. If we replace the first sentence with "The study of global governance is a very exceptional idea," we might agree that its origins (in terms of both what we study and when we decided to start studying it) are uncertain. We are handicapped by bad style – theoretically and empirically, not to mention jargon-laden prose.

But we scarcely worry about it, because the truth is that demand for global governance outstrips supply. However, because we are not clear about what exactly global governance is or how it should be understood, there appears to be no plot. This, in turn, means that every event, happening, process, and moment can be, and often is, invoked as part of the continuing scholarly theater. It is worth pursuing nevertheless!

Orwell's review of *The Good Earth* is a light-hearted way of underscoring the seriousness with which we should clarify the contours of global governance as an intellectual pursuit and why we should desist from the illusion that it is functioning effectively. In the quarter century since the foundation of the first global public policy journal to bear its name, global governance as a field of study remains ambiguously defined and uncertainly prosecuted. We do not yet have a settled understanding, a clearly defined terrain, commonly identifiable subjects, or a bespoke theoretical canon. Certainly, observers have made similar claims about international relations as an academic discipline.[2] Yet, while IR scholars have at least agreed to disagree – taking a measure of solace from the discipline's argumentative character[3] – global governance has not been subjected to the same kind of robust debate. The result is that the various components of what global governance might be rattle around in a mental box making very little sense but a lot of noise in conferences, workshops, and policy forums. Is it any wonder that the study of global governance, like the world itself, is in disarray?[4]

A rattling box may be satisfactory for some, but it impedes global governance from realizing its potential as an analytical device and an intellectual and real-world pursuit. It also undermines the value that global governance may have as an optic on wider world politics, our capacity to think about progressive global change, and our formulation of better global public policy. So, how do we go about changing this state of affairs? Our claim is that, to respond meaningfully to the challenge of making global governance fit for purpose, we need to go back to basics and seek answers to three foundational questions: What is global governance? When did it start? What exactly is "global" about global governance? We need answers to these questions if we are to understand exactly the nature of the beast and how to tame it. Further, we need to add a fourth and seldom asked question: How is global governance encountered, not only by those that receive it but also by those domains (natural and otherwise) over which its effects are felt? Only then can we make serious advances in thinking about how we can effect desirable change.

This introductory chapter outlines why we believe it is essential to go back to basics if we are to make headway in rendering global governance more analytically attractive. We offer some preliminary comments for each of the four preceding questions and then tease out answers in detail in the chapters that follow. Our purpose throughout is to clarify the contours of global governance as a field and to reflect upon – as well as add precision to – scholarship that may have the capacity to underpin better public policy. We hope to avoid what Orwell decried as "slovenliness" and "euphemism, question-begging and sheer cloudy vagueness" in the use of language and to parse some basics, including the use of global governance as an optic on world orders past and present, the role of power therein, and how we might account for growing global complexity.[5] We cannot promise to have rescued global governance from the edge of the abyss; but we hope at least to have cast out a lifeline worthy of grasping.

What is Global Governance?

Two almost simultaneous events ignited scholarly interest in global governance. The first consisted of the project to understand better the changing shape of worldwide governance in the wake of thawing East-West tensions. The second was the normative endeavor to work out how the world could be governed more effectively in the immediate post-Cold War era. The driving motivation in the first was how to understand and manage global complexity. Here scholars sought to work out how governance operated on a global scale without formal authority; the precise nature of world order's new complexion; how we might think theoretically about global governance; the interconnections between its various "levels" (local, national, regional, and planetary); and what viable alternatives might be.[6]

The onset of the post-Cold War era thus focused analytical attention on making the best use of existing global governance machinery – however primitive – after the disappearance of the paralyzing tendencies of superpower rivalry. Foremost in the minds of scholars and practitioners was finding ways to make it possible for the United Nations (UN) finally to realize its potential in the provision of global public goods.[7] At the same time, there was a widespread recognition that significant gaps existed in UN capacity along with the number and complexity of the challenges facing not only the world organization but also humanity as a whole. In addition, there was a notable pluralization in the number of actors visibly engaged on the world stage. The result was that advocates of hybrid governance and devolved management sought to harness the potential of non-state actors – from both civil society and the for-profit sector – under the umbrella

5

and oversight of multilateral organizations, and especially of the UN system. These hybrid instances of governance took multiple forms, including the UN Global Compact; the subcontracting arrangements between the UN and regional organizations for security operation and non-governmental organizations (NGOs) for delivery of assistance; the Internet Corporation for Assigned Names and Numbers (ICANN); and the Global Fund to Fight AIDS, Tuberculosis and Malaria, among many others.[8]

After the initial flurry of activity – and leaving aside conspiratorial commentaries[9] – the study of global governance gave way to works that increasingly treated the term as a synonym for international organizations and their capacity to deliver public goods with or without stirring non-state actors (primarily NGOs) into the pot.[10] The policy take-up treated global governance as the next big idea but in reality used it as a proxy term for international coordination in trade, climate, finance, security, and the like. The result was to generate a convergence in the understanding of both the phrase and the area of study as one focused on international organizations alone and to define global governance simply as the capacity within the international system at any moment to provide government-like services in the absence of a world government. The result was to offer little insight into how the world was formerly and is currently governed.

What went wrong? Part of the problem was a relative lack of attention to the output end of the global governance equation – that is, what did it produce? Here we need to distinguish between what global governance produces as a general phenomenon in contrast to specific or discrete instances of global public policy, coordination, and control. As a general phenomenon, global governance is the sum of all of the forces that together combine to produce and manage world order. These range from ideas about how the world is best ordered (or, as has often been the case, ordered in ways that suit the interests of the rich and powerful), through formal and informal state and non-state institutions, to market mechanisms and technological innovations. Casting our intellectual net widely in this fashion is different from a specific aspect, moment, or incidence of global governance, which assumes typically that it is international governance without government, along with the output generated. Here we might think of those UN-centered processes that resulted in the adoption of the *Transforming our World by 2030* agenda and the accompanying Sustainable Development Goals (SDGs). The general and the specific are of course connected – the agenda and the SDGs will inevitably affect the shape of world order, at present and in the immediate future. However, one is macro, holistic, and operates for the *longue durée*, whereas the other is meso, discrete, and more temporally specific. It is fair to say that scholarly endeavors in the past quarter century have been concerned primarily with the temporally specific aspects of global governance – understood as contemporary demand for, and supply of, global public policy[11] – rather than with understanding the production and management of world orders.

A crucial consequence of the paucity of attention to the output side of the global governance equation is how we understand continuity and change – that is, the essence of comprehending the nature and pace of alterations in patterns over time. It also has a bearing on how we understand time and space in global governance as well as how we might answer the question "When did it start?" The appreciation of continuity and change as a general phenomenon requires an aggregated assessment. This, in turn, requires understanding how governance arrangements hold together, the substance of their ideological content, and the relations of power that underpin them. Detecting what drives change and what ensures continuity in global governance is different from what encourages adjustments or the maintenance of policies and practices in discrete instances. These broader brushstrokes conform to understanding continuity and change at different levels and enable us to understand, as well as to draw distinctions between, changes *of* global governance – that is, in its overall arrangement – and changes *in* global governance – modest adjustments that may be noteworthy or not, depending on the character of the system in place. Issues of continuity and change, and changes *of* and *in* global governance, are key to our attempts to rescue global governance from a simple association with one specific post-Cold War moment as well as the actions and activities of international organizations. These are central themes throughout these pages.

When Did it Start?

As we have seen, distinguishing between global governance as a general phenomenon and its discrete aspects puts us in a position to characterize changes of grand arrangements and more particularly alternations therein. Understanding global governance as a general phenomenon (and the changes undergone) requires that we trace the mechanisms for the management of world order back in time, noting that the distinctions between epochs are marked by fundamental transitions in arrangement. These transitions need not be dramatic breaks with the past – indeed, they may result from the aggregation of minor adjustments or long and messy periods of flux – but they should constitute clear departures from earlier systems of management. Such departures may at first glance be ambiguous and discernible only after extended periods and with the benefit of hindsight. However, they are predicated on the assumption that global governance is not just a contemporary phenomenon but, rather, has existed in one form or another for some time.

A good illustration would be the distinction between (and the transition from), on the one hand, the long nineteenth-century system of world order management underpinned by European domination, governed through complex diplomatic intercourse, and organized around principles of empire, hierarchy, and racial discrimination and, on the other hand, the partial twentieth-century arrangement founded on US–Soviet conflict, governed by multilateral institutions, regional organizations, and composite bilateral arrangements and organized on principles of the market and the commune.[12] In this example, change was driven by those forces that affected the general arrangement of global governance (ideology, material power, relative capabilities) and that triggered a transition from the long nineteenth-century to the short twentieth-century version of global governance.

This change *of* global governance is different from a change *in* global governance, with, for example, the move from the 2000–2015 Millennium Development Goals (MDGs) to their successor 2016–2030 Sustainable Development Goals (SDGs) as the foci for global development governance. In this latter example, understanding change requires a forensic appreciation of global public policy processes and alterations to the context in which those processes took place, whereas the former example encourages us to stand back and ask questions about the production and governance of world order. That said, a robust understanding of the discrete aspects of global governance also requires an appreciation of its overall – that is, its system-wide – arrangements. In other words, we cannot fully appreciate global governance by examining only one part. A comprehension of its grand formation is required to situate it within an appropriate context and determine whether the transition is distinct enough to constitute a change *of* rather than merely a change *in* global governance.

This approach has a bearing on establishing when global governance actually began. At the level of a general phenomenon, global governance begins when world orders emerge. In this way, it is concerned with the arrangement and management of world order. Thus, understanding change therein requires us to comprehend how world orders emerge and are governed as well as what drives clear departures from preceding patterns of management. We have yet to comprehend fully this task; we have not mapped epochal changes in global governance systems over millennia; indeed, we are overwhelmed in imagining such an undertaking.[13]

It could be said that contemporary global governance (that is, the epoch in which we currently live) begins with the end of World War II, although architectural sketches of its foundations were drawn after World War I. Certainly key developments have occurred since 1945, but its overall form and character have not yet altered significantly. For instance, while the way that global exchange rates are managed and financial markets operate and are governed has changed significantly over the course of the current era, the dominant relations of power underpinning the system have remained largely untouched. This does not mean that significant power alternations have been absent – to which the demise of the Soviet Union and the "rise" of China and of other emerging powers, among others, attest. However, it does mean that the end of the Bretton Woods system of fixed exchange rates, the transition from the General Agreement on Tariffs and Trade (GATT) to the World Trade Organization (WTO), and the metamorphosis of the Organisation for European Economic Co-operation into the Organisation for Economic Co-operation and Development (OECD) are all changes within the current global governance epoch, as is the emergence of an array of new actors and mechanisms that now have a major effect on the shape of world order, including the activities of these organizations.[14] Thus, while understanding what has driven these changes in the present system is important, they are temporally bound because they are features of one prevailing world order. To understand how and why that order came about, we need also to appreciate the causes of wider systemic change as well as the relationship between that overall change in arrangement and the discrete developments that subsequently occurred – such as those outlined above – and which preceded its transition.

What Exactly is "Global" about Global Governance?

Appreciating what drives change at different levels by framing our understanding temporally is not, however, the only consequence of distinguishing between different forms of global governance. We need also to think in spatial terms about differences in scale between systems. Conceptualizing global governance as the arrangement and management of world order not only requires looking back in time before we have previously imagined; it also necessitates liberating "global" from the assumption that it has necessarily to connote "planetary" space. Thus, global governance refers to the sum of all of the forces that combine to give coherence to a particular world order at any specific moment in time. This aggregation may be genuinely planetary, as global governance is today, but it may also be less widespread, as it was in previous epochs. What matters is to capture the sum of the elements that combine to lend order to and help orchestrate significant portions of the world.

The insistence that "global" must be "planetary" has so far prevented global governance from having analytical purchase beyond the moment in which we live. The tendency is to assume that, because our era is the first to have institutions, technologies, and policies that purport to be global and to touch every corner of the world, only now are we actually able to peer through the lenses of "global" governance. Yet, what is truly distinctive about the current world order is that it is the first to be defined by total human domination of the planet (that is, we have entered the Anthropocene).[15] Previous formations of global governance produced world orders that physically encompassed less than the entire planet. However, they were still "global" in the sense that they were widespread enough to encompass many, if not the most isolated, elements of humanity even if their coverage was not worldwide. Few could suggest that European imperialism was not the primary means by which nineteenth-century world order was organized and governed – or the global governance of that time. Yet significant portions of the globe were not under colonial control, and the variations in imperial operating procedures among the competing empires were consequential. Hence, we should acknowledge that other systems of governance, control, and domination at other times were the means by which earlier epochs were ordered and by which the global governance of that day operated.

How is it Received?

We need to put in place one more piece of our puzzle if we are to begin to appreciate global governance more completely, as well as how we might bring about desirable change. It is striking to note how much work on global governance is unidirectional; it focuses on events at the top of the world's food chain and how they flow downwards (if at all). Very few scholars have explored how global governance is received, encountered, and experienced – not just by humans but by the natural world as well.[16] This is a significant shortcoming in our analytical enterprise. In the current era, much of the practice of global governance originates in the industrial and technological heartlands of the Western hemisphere. Yet, in key areas the vast majority of the recipients of global governance are in the Global South. It is also striking, for instance, that some of the world's most precarious communities have a more direct and intimate familiarity with global governance via the complex web of development agencies than do citizens of the United Kingdom or the United States. The same can be said for complexes of health and other financial actors of which the primary intergovernmental institutions – the World Bank, International Monetary Fund (IMF), and World Health Organization (WHO) – are just part.

This perspective is further refined when we consider that in some contexts the impact of these policies and programs is even more acutely experienced by women, children, the elderly, and indigenous communities. Yet, these vantage points are seldom visible when we think about the design, consequence, or conception of global governance.[17] Moreover, precisely because we have tended to study global governance in this unidirectional fashion, we evaluate its successes and failures from on high. Yet, doing so commits the same mistakes as the tourist in Jamaica Kincaid's *A Small Place* – that is, of adopting a vantage point that cannot hope to understand the lives, circumstances, and consequences that are being observed.[18] We need to refine this optic considerably if we are to design better global governance.

Where Are We?

When we think about today's global governance and of the adjustments and alterations that we may wish to make, an essential challenge is to understand how to synchronize its discrete aspects with the overall management of world order, the planetary with the local, and power with powerlessness. We have to keep our eye on the longer-run consequences of what are – temporally speaking – short-term policy proposals and the places from which they are viewed and received. It also means that, in paying attention to the output end of the equation – that is, the resulting world order – we focus on how global governance was, is, and will be received. It also means that we must consider how initiatives in the here and now influence the general shape of world order down the road.

To return to the author whose work we used as an entry point to our discussion, Orwell had something more to say that illustrates well the consequences that discrete aspects of global governance can have in determining the main characteristics of an epoch.

In reflecting on the United Nations Organization (UNO) only six months after its formal creation in 1945, he lamented:

> In order to have any efficacy whatever, a world organization must be able to override big states as well as small ones. It must have [the] power to inspect and limit armaments, which means that its officials must have access to every square inch of every country. It must also have at its disposal an armed force bigger than any other armed force . . . responsible only to the organization itself. The two or three great states that really matter have never even pretended to agree to any of these conditions, and they have so arranged the constitution of U.N.O. that their own actions cannot even be discussed. In other words, U.N.O.'s usefulness as an instrument of world peace is nil.[19]

Orwell's is an important reminder. While particular global governance initiatives may be, or appear to be, worthy they will have little progressive effect, now or in the longer term, if they serve mainly to cement new or perpetuate existing problematic, exploitive, and unfair systems as the UNO did. This is why in thinking analytically about global governance we have chosen to highlight the necessity of bringing the normative back to the fore.

Thus, our attempt in the chapters that follow is to push for a wholesale rethinking of global governance so that claims that there are possibilities only for piecemeal solutions in global public policy no longer hold. We begin in the next chapter by probing further the problématique of global governance. Our aim is to show how and why we have gotten global governance so wrong, why it does not have to be this way, and where we can sensibly go from here. In chapters 2, 3, and 4 we parse the aspects of the global governance puzzle just introduced. Chapter 2 makes the case for using global governance as a device for exploring world orders past, present, and future. Chapter 3 disrupts the common association between global governance and planetary management by drawing attention to the spread and expansion of world orders across the Earth through time. Chapter 4 sets out why a concern with global governance can no longer be a top-down affair alone by exploring the necessity of taking account of its everyday manifestations. Chapter 5 sets out why we believe that our approach may enable us to improve how we think about and practice global governance. While we are unable to solve all of the problems that world order and its governance present, we conclude nonetheless that we will at least have more secure analytical moorings.

1

The Global Governance Problématique

In the opening pages we noted that a settled understanding of the term "global governance" remains elusive. This is perhaps not surprising given that, after a little over a quarter of a century since the term was first coined, it has come to be interpreted in so many ways. After all, as Fernand Braudel noted, the "vocabulary of the social sciences . . . scarcely permits decisive definitions." Instead, "there are wide and frequent variations in the meaning of the simplest words, according to the thought that uses and informs them." His view was that "most expressions, far from being fixed for ever, vary from one author to another, and continually evolve before our eyes."[1]

The contested nature of the meaning of global governance stands in marked contrast to understandings of governance at the local, national, and regional level. Here, talk of governance is bound up with, and has evolved from, a perceived movement away from the state as the primary actor engaged in the act of governing to a situation in which concerts of actors are increasingly drawn together to provide more effective and widespread modes of governance, as well as to make up for the shortcomings of state-only forms of administration and delivery.[2] These organizational forms are infused with a new public management ethos heavily reliant on notions of subsidiarity and marketization; and the challenge is to increase the accountability and perhaps the legitimacy of the various non-state actors involved.

At the global level these developments are not quite so discernible. While it might be the case that a range of actors are now active on the world stage, plotting at the global level the kinds of movements that have occurred at other levels is made problematic by the absence of an overarching political entity. Matters are compounded by a disciplinary reluctance in international relations to consider just how much authority is wielded by non-state actors in a field of study traditionally focused on states and a tenacity that has seen scholars defend the integrity of the state as the primary actor and principal source of authority on the world stage.[3] For many, global governance is held up to be little more than intellectual fad and fancy, a woolly term that adds little to the political science lexicon, an oxymoron, or a smoke-screen under which plots for a world government and global polity can be smuggled.[4] For others, it is a serious concept to be engaged and interrogated, though – as we have noted – little agreement exists as to its precise content.[5]

There are, nevertheless, empirical realities that push us to think harder about – or at least make it harder to ignore – various elements of global governance. In so doing, they press us into thinking about how better global governance might be realized. We need, for instance, to take seriously public perceptions and empirical realities that decision-making is increasingly taken up by (and sometimes ceded to) a wide variety of actors (international institutions, transnational corporations, think tanks, foundations, business associations, international conferences, and the like). At the same time, we need to account for the centrifugal tendencies that are unravelling integration processes the world over. In the EU and some of its member states, as well as elsewhere, we are witnessing the erosion of the previously firm foundations of fledgling intergovernmental and supranational efforts to build the global governance that we currently have; and we see increasing grit in the already gridlocked machinery of international negotiations.[6]

Our attention is also required to understand better the consequences of the increasing role of financial markets not just in shaping political decision-making but also in everyday life; the impact of trade negotiations, intellectual property rights regimes, and development financing on the economic fortunes of developing countries; the influence of business activities on the health of the local, national, regional, and global environments; the growth of regional and global legal and standard-setting machineries; the emergence of transnational criminal, terrorist, mercenary, and paramilitary organizations; the interplay between, and role of, NGOs of all varieties (from the internationally active to the grassroots); and the pressures to address the failures of contemporary global governance to attenuate a raft of such destabilizing issues as growing disparities in income, wealth, and human health, accelerating climate change, intractable conflict, genocide, and mass human rights violations.

In the face of such complexity – indeed, confusion – we also need to resist the temptation to talk about pursuing better global governance by simply increasing the participation of developing countries and non-state interests in the global institutions that we incorrectly assume are the sum of global governance. They are not. Instead, we need to begin from an understanding that, individually, these actors, the mechanisms through which substantial global governance is currently exercised, and the outcomes that they produce shape all aspects of global life. Together they represent elements and agents involved in the construction of world order. As such, we should seek to comprehend better both the various ways that shape is given to the current order and how that order is being (re)negotiated, refined, and recast, as well as where it came from and where it is headed. Only then can we begin to think about "better" global governance, a central task in the final chapter of this book.

This first chapter begins with a discussion of the four primary pursuits that we believe help us conceive and apply global governance in a more satisfactory fashion. It then takes a closer look at the intellectual genesis of the term "global governance," concentrating on why it emerged, what it was intended to depict, and how its meaning has evolved over the last quarter century. We show how its appearance was linked to a specific set of changes in authority and the exercise of power that became visible at the end of the twentieth and the beginning of the twenty-first century. We note that, while the term arose to describe turmoil in the late twentieth century, its association with that specific moment has frozen it in time and deprived it of greater purchase. Put another way, "global governance" has come to mean world governance without world government. Instead, it should be interpreted as a more purposeful analytical tool for appreciating how the globe is organized and world orders fashioned in the past, present, and future.

Thereafter, we explore what global governance has helped us explain, but also what it has missed. Our claim is that imprecision has resulted in a feebler conceptual tool than it could be for understanding how the world is organized and power wielded therein. By way of a correction, we then spell out four desirable components of an investigation into the organization and governance of world orders. The penultimate section considers how, despite its emergence from – and indeed its relationship with – a specific and quite recent historical moment, global governance has considerable analytical traction in looking further back. It can provide insights to explain the nature and complexities of, as well as wholesale changes in, previous world orders, and also to look forward to how the contemporary and future world might and ought to be organized.

Four Pursuits

Our principal aim in the following pages is to press for a wholesale rethinking of how we conceive and apply the term so that it has practical, conceptual, and normative value. On the one hand, "global governance" has become both widespread and useful for describing growing complexity in the way that the world is organized and authority exercised as well as shorthand for referring to a collection of institutions with planetary reach. On the other hand, analysts have not mined the term sufficiently to provide either a better handle on what the sum of these discrete elements of global governance produce or the underlying dynamics of change and continuity. A deeper investigation of contemporary global governance should capture how power is used worldwide and how a multiplicity of actors relate to one another generally, as well as on specific issues. It should also make better sense of growing global complexity and account for alterations in the way that the world is and has been organized and governed over time – both within and among historical periods.

Our contention is that an investigation into global governance should concentrate on four primary pursuits. First, it should move beyond the strong association between the term and virtually any change in the late twentieth and early twenty-first centuries. It should instead be understood that the complexities of the post-Cold War era are concrete expressions of contemporary global governance, but that formations of global governance have been and will be different in other epochs. Second, it should identify and explain the structure of global authority, accounting not just for grand patterns of command and control but also for how regional, national, and local systems intersect with and push against that structure. Third, a central preoccupation should be to investigate the myriad ways that power is exercised within such a system, how interests are articulated and pursued, and the kind of ideas and discourses from which power and interests draw substance as well as which help establish, maintain, and perpetuate the system. Fourth, it should account for changes *in* and *of* the system and focus on the causes, consequences, and drivers of change and continuity, not just today but over extended periods in the past and into the future.

To reiterate, in embarking on these four pursuits, our aim at this juncture is not to advance a comprehensive theory of global governance. Rather, it is to highlight where core questions should encourage us to go. To help us along the way, we start with earlier work that has fallen by the wayside and use it to re-energize the search for a better understanding of – as Martin Hewson and Timothy Sinclair put it – "global governance as it has been, is, and may become."[7] Our hope is that, if some of our propositions are correct, and if better answers to the questions that global governance encourages us to ask are forthcoming, a more rigorous conception should help us begin to understand better the nature of the contemporary phenomenon as well as look "backwards" and "forwards." Such an investigation should provide historical insights and prescriptive elements to appreciate the kind of world order that we ought to be seeking and encourage us to investigate how that global governance can come about. The value-added results from opening our eyes to how the world was, is, will be, and ought to be organized – this last being particularly pertinent and certainly better than simply "muddling through"[8] as we seek to counter the threats that confront the planet.

The Emergence of Global Governance

The term "global governance" was born from a marriage – neither shotgun nor arranged but precipitated by a blend of real-world events and developments in the academy – between academic theory and practical policy formulation in the 1990s and became entwined with that other meta-phenomenon of the last two decades, globalization. James Rosenau and Ernst Czempiel's theoretical *Governance without Government* was published in 1992, just about the same time that the Swedish government launched the policy-oriented Commission on Global Governance with Sonny Ramphal and Ingmar Carlsson as co-chairs. Both set in motion interest in the newly coined notion of "global governance." The 1995 publication of the commission's report, *Our Global Neighbourhood*, coincided with the first issue of the

23

Academic Council on the United Nations System's journal *Global Governance*. This quarterly sought to return to the global problem-solving origins of the leading journal in the field, *International Organization*, which seemed to have lost its way. As Timothy Sinclair puts it, "From the late 1960s, the idea of international organization fell into disuse . . . [and] *International Organization*, the journal which carried this name founded in the 1940s, increasingly drew back from matters of international policy and instead became a vehicle for the development of rigorous academic theorizing."[9]

These developments paved the way for a raft of works about growing global complexity, the management of globalization, and the challenges confronting international institutions.[10] The collective means of talking about them became global governance. But global governance also replaced an immediate predecessor as a normative endeavor, "world order studies," which was seen as overly top-down and static. Having grown from *World Peace through World Law* – the classic text from Grenville Clark and Louis Sohn – world order failed to capture the variety of actors, networks, and relationships that characterized contemporary international relations.[11] When the perspectives from world order scholars began to look a little old-fashioned, the stage was set for a new analytical and normative cottage industry.

After his archival labors to write a two-volume history of world federalism, Joseph Barrata aptly observed that, in the 1990s, "the new expression, 'global governance,' emerged as an acceptable term in debate on international organization for the desired and practical goal of progressive efforts, in place of 'world government.'" Scholars, he continued, "wished to avoid using a term that would harken back to the thinking about world government in the 1940s, which was largely based on fear of atomic bombs and too often had no practical proposals for the transition short of a revolutionary act of the united peoples of the world."[12] Michael Barnett and Raymond Duvall put it more succinctly and adroitly: "The idea of global governance has attained near-celebrity status. In little more than a decade the concept has gone from the ranks of the unknown to one of the central orienting themes in the practice and study of international affairs."[13] Michael Zürn calculates that the growth rate of new titles for global governance now surpasses all others in international relations, and its absolute annual numbers now are greater than the more familiar "war and peace" and "international cooperation."[14]

The result was that the emergence of the term – and changes in the way that the purpose of insights from it were expressed – imbued global governance with the normative aspirations that had motivated previous generations of IR, international organization (IO), international law (IL), and international political economy (IPE) scholars. Global governance came to refer to collective efforts to identify, understand, and address worldwide problems and processes that went beyond the capacities of individual states. It included both formal *and* informal values, rules, norms, practices, and organizations that provided better order than relying purely upon formal regulations and structures. And it reflected a desire for the international system at any moment in time to provide government-like services in the absence of anything like a world government. Global governance was thus perceived to encompass a wide variety of cooperative and progressive problem-solving arrangements that were visible but informal (e.g., practices or guidelines) or were temporary formations (e.g., coalitions of the willing). Such arrangements could also be more formal, taking the shape of hard rules (laws and treaties) or institutions with administrative structures and established practices to manage collective affairs by a variety of actors – including state authorities, intergovernmental organizations (IGOs), NGOs, private-sector entities, and other civil society actors.[15]

It is also worth noting that the need to refresh thinking about international organization and future world order animated the efforts of scholars working under the auspices of the "Multilateralism and the United Nations System" (MUNS) – a project coordinated by Robert W. Cox and sponsored by the United Nations University (UNU).[16] Scholars working with the MUNS project sought to capture, revitalize, and build upon the legitimacy connoted by the term "multilateralism" as a way of thinking about how better to organize the world. While it was a more limited endeavor, in that its focus was primarily on one form of international institutionalization, it nonetheless offered a pointer on how the analytical and the normative components of global governance might be usefully separated and combined. As Cox summarized:

> "Global governance" means the procedures and practices which exist at the world (or regional) level for the management of political, economic and social affairs. One hypothetical form of governance (world government or world empire) can be conceived as having a hierarchical form of coordination, whether centralized (unitary) or decentralized (federal). The other form of coordination would be non-hierarchical, and this we would call multilateral.[17]

Earlier, John Ruggie directed a widely cited project that aimed to substantiate the idea that "multilateralism matters,"[18] albeit

26

less ambitious than MUNS in the way that it conceptualized the capacity of this institutional form to be fashioned. A later UNU project actually challenged his more traditional concept of multilateralism.[19] Yet, the insights of all of these projects were unable to rehabilitate the study of global authority via a reclaimed multilateralism. Global governance proved more pervasive as well as more persuasive.

Global governance also became associated with another normative project ignited by worries about the shortfalls in the capacity of states to rein in the activities of a range of actors as well as to blunt the sharper consequences of global marketization and the seemingly unstoppable actions of powerful international economic institutions. In this variation of what Nayan Chanda called "runaway globalization,"[20] the political authority of some great powers and international economic organizations, along with the absence of authority among others (largely those states that encountered globalization as a quasi-force of nature),[21] underpinned growing civil society dissatisfaction.[22] This disgruntlement found expression in mass demonstrations during the meetings of the WTO, IMF, World Bank, EU, and various regional development banks, as well as in the growth of an anti- and then an alter-globalization movement.[23] The result was a pressure for globalization "with a human face" accompanied by a global governance to match.[24]

In short, potential analytical traction disappeared because global governance meant so many different things to so many different people. It embodied the hopes and fears of many inside and outside the academy at the turn of the millennium. Yet, it failed to satisfy the need to analyze those tumultuous times.

Plus ça change . . .

For all of the interest generated by growing complexity, as well as its manifestation in novel thinking about global governance, old ways persisted. Three-quarters of a century of distinguishing the study of IR from political science as one characterized by a focus on states as the primary units of analysis continued to condition and constrain thinking and weighed heavily on the way that scholars understood this altered world.[25] Specialists in IO and IL continued to emphasize the role of major powers in intergovernmental bodies as the central lens through which to view world politics – how else to analyze organizations whose member states determine the agenda and sometimes pay the bills?

However, older ways sometimes also involved thinking outside of these boxes. Harold Jacobson observed much earlier that the march by states toward a world government was woven into the tapestries decorating the walls of the Palais des Nations in Geneva – now the UN's European Office but earlier the headquarters of the first international experiment that aspired to universal state membership, the defunct League of Nations. These images "picture the process of humanity combining into ever larger and more stable units for the purpose of governance – first the family, then the tribe, then the city-state, and then the nation – a process which presumably would eventually culminate in the planet being combined into a single political unit."[26] While many are now skeptical that this is where humanity is heading any time soon, calls for and engagements with the idea of world government have not fallen entirely by the wayside[27] – even if scholars such as Mark Mazower are comfortable with the disappearance of this idea.[28]

Thus, our best shot was to use the label "global governance" for this complex world where authority was exercised differently but to persist in familiar state-centric ways of understanding it, to view other actors and activities as appendages to the international system that analysts have observed and debated since the Peace of Westphalia. What the ups and downs of global change had injected was curiosity and some new questions. They revolved around how the world was organized and authority and power exercised therein, with the acknowledgement that we missed part of the action by merely peering at states. We nonetheless stopped short of providing real answers to questions that pushed us beyond comfort levels with older modes of thinking.

According to Craig Murphy's masterful history of "global governance" *avant la lettre* since the middle of the nineteenth century, international organizations are customarily viewed as "what world government we actually have."[29] He is right, but the problem lies elsewhere. At the national level, we have the authoritative structures of government that governance supplements. However, internationally we simply have governance with some architectural drawings for modest renovations in international structures that are several decades old and not up to present building codes. Detailed blueprints sit in filing cabinets, while unstable ground and foundations shift under feeble existing structures. Meanwhile, a host of other actors, processes, and mechanisms often occupy too much of our peripheral vision and distract our attention. The result has been to reduce the value of global governance in understanding complexity and especially the drivers of change and continuity.

We also have too closely associated the term with attempts to explain the particular moment in time that catalyzed the post-Cold War era. That existing international organizations cannot address pressing contemporary challenges is evident from their demonstrated inability to bind key states in meaningful ways to address global problems – fledgling efforts to protect the natural environment, eradicate world poverty, or attenuate increasing inequalities within and across states and social groups bear ample witness. Consequently, the association of global governance with the hopes, worries, and complexities of a particular moment runs the risk of making the concept a relic, if it has not done so already. This consignment brings with it a risk of losing sight of questions about how the world is organized and authority exercised, now or ever. In short, we need to rescue the term.

Reviving Global Governance

These risks should push us to probe more deeply into how the world truly is organized – or, as Ruggie suggested some time ago, how the world hangs together.[30] What is required for us to realize the analytical utility of global governance? The first part of an answer is to tackle global complexity in a more satisfactory fashion, not to be afraid to disaggregate by issue and by context, and then to try to fit what we find back together into a better explanatory whole. We should describe not only who the actors are and how they connect to one another but also how a particular outcome has resulted and why and on what grounds authority is effectively or poorly exercised. We should examine the consequences of new forms of organization and determine what adjustments might enhance their utility to meet existing, new, or changing objectives. Important as well are subtler understandings and a better appreciation of the differing characteristics of actors, institutions, and governance machineries and their importance when those with varying natures and capabilities come together or clash.

Another essential task is to give greater thought to the way that power is exercised. This has to be a more nuanced endeavor than simply indicating that Germany is not Gabon, that "emerging" powers are on the rise, or that the end of *Pax Americana* may be nigh.[31] In today's international system, state capabilities matter, but so too does the way that formal and informal institutions mediate relations between states and the way that goods and services are exchanged and managed. When the numbers and kinds of actors proliferate, when states exert less control over markets, and when complex relations exist among various actors and markets, questions of power are less straightforward. Here we should probe more than the relationship between the birth of the current phase of international institutions and US power, illustrated by the insightful work of Ruggie and John Ikenberry.[32] We should also reflect on institutional expressions and social groups, epistemic communities and policy networks, and financial decision-making and changing capabilities among other actors.[33]

Finally, and despite some notable endeavors,[34] we have yet to understand fully the ideas and interests that drive the machineries of governance that we have and, more particularly, how they arose and developed and, subsequently, permeated and modified the international system at all levels. Here ideas themselves are crucial, as are the value systems upon which they sit and which they inform, the discourses in which they are embedded, and the interests to which they speak. So too are the entrepreneurs who generate ideas, the networks through which they are disseminated, the ways that various institutions mediate core messages, and the processes through which they are translated into forms of organization and policy delivery. So far, we have failed to link adequately ideas to global governance, to tease out what works and why. The result is that we have fallen short of answering Jeffrey Checkel's call for "mid-level theory."[35]

Without a concerted effort to press forward our understanding of the complexities of global governance, the way that authority and power are exercised, and the ideational and material aspects of world order, we risk not only misunderstanding but also underestimating our capacity to make meaningful adjustments to that order and its governance. In short, we can no longer ignore global governance's unrealized potential to help explain change and continuity – past, present, and future.

Global Governance: Backwards and Forwards

Thinking harder about global governance may have utility beyond understanding where we are and the nature of the world order in which we live, or which actors we should or should not emphasize or ignore.[36] Certainly, some of the questions asked in the closing decades of the twentieth century may be useful in helping us understand where we have come from and where we are going – in the words of Thomas Hale, David Held, and Kevin Young, we need to appreciate the dynamics of the partial successes that have led to "gridlock" versus those that have moved "beyond."[37] But we also need to push the analytical utility of global governance's range as a conceptual device beyond the current order and the ideas advanced about a refashioned multilateralism immediately after the Cold War's demise.

Earlier we recalled Robert Cox's distinction between forms of global governance – in his case, as multilateralism and as world government or empire. This distinction provides a potentially fruitful way of thinking about global governance which removes some of the blinkers that its association with the post-Cold War moment imposes. Currently configured, we understand global governance as the sum of the informal and formal ideas, values, norms, procedures, and institutions that help all actors – states, IGOs, civil society, NGOs, transnational corporations, and the like – identify, makes sense of, and address transboundary problems. Yet, our analytical view must go beyond its *contemporary* manifestations, which emerged from a specific and recent historical moment and which responded to a perceived need to understand the surprises and disarray that followed upon what had seemed, temporarily, such positive changes after the end of East–West tensions.

Pursuing answers to questions about how the world is governed across time should also give us a better idea about where we have come from, why change or continuity resulted, and where we are or, even better, could be going. Put differently, we should adapt the same kinds of questions that led to our initial understanding of global governance as the pluralization of world politics amid a growing array of complex problems at the end of the last century. If so, we should also be able to determine what kinds of systems of world order existed before the current one and how power and authority were employed. In brief, we should have improved answers about the ultimate drivers of change and continuity.

A willingness to ask how the world was governed as well as how that governance has changed over time has the potential to shake up thinking about IR more broadly. It destabilizes conventional wisdom and opens our analytical aspirations to examine complexities that, in fact, have existed for some time. As many have shown, the "global governance" of the Westphalian era – although not so labelled by most analysts – was more than an anarchic state system. At the dawn of the post-Cold War era, Hendrik Spruyt reminded us that a host of actors – states as well as non-state actors – had always been involved in global governance, although states have by far tended to be the more capable and powerful actors.[38]

Perhaps the best that we can say is that we have manufactured a handle to grasp how the interstate part of the global governance complex has worked over the last half-century. However, we have spent too little time researching what other agents and forms of governance exist and have existed and what their relationships have been with the interstate system – not just in the last few decades but for centuries.

One way of thinking about global governance over time is to evaluate prevailing ideas about world order at any given moment. In the two-dimensional and static view of the Westphalian order as essentially an interstate system, an assertion that the organizing principle is anarchy tells us little about why the world has been organized that way or why we should strive to understand what existed before. Such an approach takes us into well-charted territory, but our way of journeying through it – if we focus on questions of how and why the world is organized – is different and potentially more insightful.

One reason for the emergence of the interstate system as the broad framework that governs the world was a response to ideas that – in the European world at least – sought to move away from a form of governance in which papal authority was supreme to one in which various secular and non-secular rulers exercised sovereignty over discrete geographic units. While ideas of self-determination found their first expression here, the move from papacy to state was not necessarily in the interests of those populations who were subjected to previous or subsequent forms of governance. Nor did it end the influence of the papacy - or of religious institutions more generally - in the global governance of that time or extinguish ideas about the subjugation of peoples beyond notional national borders as a "legitimate" product of that global governance.

Other agents that contributed to how the world was governed until this point - such as mercenary armies and city-states, to name but two - fell into relative desuetude, but new actors emerged to play more central roles. The age of empire, as described in Eric Hobsbawm's book of that title,[39] came about, for instance, in part through the actions and activities of private enterprises - which in many cases started off as "privateer" ventures and became the nationally sanctioned "companies" of European empires - and the role they played in extending imperialism as a worldwide system of order and governance. Thus, asking questions about the rush to empire enables us to see the role of such actors as the British and the Dutch East India companies. It also helps to distinguish between the kind of global governance that existed before and during the accumulation of European imperial power (as well as the brutal forms of governance experience by colonized peoples) and the versions that existed once the scramble for territory subsided and the world map had settled into areas demarcated by colonial acquisition and expansion.

Our usual disciplinary route into thinking about how the world was organized and ordered in the nineteenth century is to examine how the balance of power was institutionalized among the major European states through the Holy Alliance and the Concert of Europe.[40] Yet this perspective merely tells us of efforts to avoid costly and catastrophic wars in Europe, not how the world was governed. Absent are the competing imperialisms that were the dominant frame of nineteenth-century global governance along with differing ideas about the subjugation of non-European peoples and the colonization of apparently uninhabited lands (treated as *terra nullius* irrespective of indigenous populations). Also missing are the ways that this dominant form of organization and its ideas were challenged – both ideationally and physically – which in turn eroded the bases of competing imperialisms and helped set in motion wholesale changes in global governance.

Craig Murphy's examination of international public unions as the forerunners of the intergovernmental elements of contemporary global governance is anomalous to some because the term arose, as we have seen, early in the 1990s.[41] However, his effort suggests the crucial importance of testing the framework of global governance as an approach to understanding how the world was ordered in historical periods other than in the post-Cold War moment. The utility of Murphy's work lies in his willingness to connect changes in the form and function of contemporary global governance with the onset, consolidation, and acceleration of another global dynamic that mainstream IR has always found difficult to comprehend – the onset of the industrial revolution and the spread of capitalist production and organization.

A few other analysts have peered through these economic and social lenses as a starting point for thinking about how the world is and was organized and governed in earlier times.[42] These works contribute considerably to our understanding of the world authority structures that we actually have, but they do not – attempts to historicize these approaches further notwithstanding[43] – fully explore the kinds of questions an inquiry into the historical manifestations of global governance demands. Likewise, John M. Hobson's work on the contribution of non-Western civilizations and non-European forms of organization to the contemporary world offers useful insights into – but not a complete platform for – thinking about historical and contemporary aspects of global governance often ignored.[44]

If the need to understand change and new horizons in the immediate post-Cold War era drove us to pose questions and define contemporary global governance pluralistically, it should also encourage us to ask similar questions about earlier epochs and find satisfactory or at least better answers than we have fashioned to date. The call of historians to learn lessons for the future from the past resonates here.[45] As E. H. Carr commented, history is an "unending dialogue between the past and the present."[46] The relevance of this call was immediately obvious to three authors of an IR text, who argue that "One of the often-perceived problems of the social sciences is their lack of historical depth."[47] All too often a premium is put on the pursuit of parsimony in international relations, an endeavor that excessively values deriving and establishing the simplest of theoretical pictures and causal mechanisms. History complicates matters, which is one of the reasons why the post-Cold War vision of global governance that has come to be received wisdom appears a peculiar product. Indeed, it is because of "a frustration with parsimony and a determination to embrace a wider set of causes"[48] that those early but now largely forgotten undertakings sought to understand global governance as more than the sum of its intergovernmental parts.

Self-doubt and reflection flow naturally from historical familiarity in a way that they do not from abstract theories. Yet, wrenching global governance from a contemporary moment and applying it historically is not enough. This shift should also help inform and anticipate tomorrow. The future-oriented value lies in treating global governance as a set of questions that enable us to work out how the world was, is, and will or could be governed, how changes in grand and not so grand patterns of governance occurred, are occurring, and *ought* to occur. Our plea is for scholars to turn to this intellectual task and reconcile the problématique of global governance as a matter of urgency.

Conclusion: And Now?

It is commonplace to state that many of the most intractable contemporary problems are transnational, ranging from climate change, migration, and pandemics to terrorism, financial instability, and proliferation of weapons of mass destruction (WMD) – and that addressing them successfully requires actions that are not unilateral, bilateral, or even multilateral but, rather, global. Everything is globalizing – that is, everything except our politics. It is necessary to alter this reality despite the fact that politics is seemingly moving in the opposite direction, of hunkering down nationally in the age of Trump and Brexit, of Putin, Modi, Erdoğan, Duterte, Orbán, Obrador, and (too many) others. They are throwbacks to earlier periods in human history. Even in the last century, politicians could be fairly confident that they could quarantine their countries from various ills, which would remain confined elsewhere. However, as global integration has deepened and transboundary threats have grown, the fate of all countries – large or small, powerful or weak – is linked to that of others. Cooperation is a prerequisite to make the most of shared opportunities and to attenuate the worst of common risks. "Make [insert country name] Great Again" is simply wrong – a zero-sum slogan for an interdependent world.

The policy authority and resources necessary for tackling such problems remain vested in individual states rather than collectively in universal institutions. The classic collective action problem is how to organize common solutions to common problems and spread costs fairly. The fundamental disconnect between the nature of a growing number of global problems and the current inadequate structures for international problem-solving and decision-making goes a long way toward explaining the fitful, tactical, and short-term local responses to challenges that require sustained, strategic, and longer-run global perspectives and action.

Can a more comprehensive framework of global governance help us to attack that basic disjuncture? Contemporary global governance is a halfway house between the international anarchy underlying orthodox IR and any overarching authority. The current generation of IGOs undoubtedly lessen transaction costs and overcome some of the structural obstacles to cooperation, including norms and rules.[49] This reality should be clear to anyone examining international responses to extreme weather incidents, or ongoing humanitarian crises for which we see a constellation of helping hands – soldiers from a variety of countries, UN organizations, large and small NGOs, and even Walmart.

Global governance certainly is not the continuation of traditional power politics. It is also not the expression of an evolutionary process leading to the formation of authoritative structures able to address contemporary or future global threats. Nor is it simply bound up with governing the economy in the *longue durée*. To speak of "governance" and not "government" is to discuss the product but not its principal producers. Agency and accountability are largely absent. In the domestic context, governance adds to government and implies shared purpose and goal orientation in addition to formal authority and police or enforcement powers. For the globe, governance is the whole story.

Our aim is to take conceptual steps toward a more complete framework of global governance. Our journey is directed toward a better understanding of how the world was and currently is organized, including how its complexity is manifest, how authority and power are exercised, what the ideational and material drivers of change and continuity are, and who benefits or loses. That knowledge should also place us in a position to propose what should and could happen to improve the planet's prospects.

At the end of the day, we require more satisfactory answers to the question "What is global governance?" Otherwise, we have images from two authors who rarely appear in scholarly journals: Gertrude Stein's characterization of Oakland – "there is no there there" – or Lewis Carroll's Cheshire cat – a grinning head floating without a body or substance.

In comparison to the study of traditional IO or IL, peering through the lens of global governance opens the analyst's eyes to viewing a host of actors and informal processes of norm and policy formulation as well as change and action. The crucial challenge in the immediate term is to push the study of global governance beyond the notion of "add actors and processes into international organization and stir."

Certainly, global problems require global solutions. This realization requires that we identify cooperation at various levels and with specific actors so that we can determine how global public goods can result from a host of means and forms, formal and informal, including a consideration of supranational authority. We can point to numerous examples of helpful steps in issue-specific global governance. For instance, we have the International Committee of the Red Cross (ICRC) for the laws of war and humanitarian principles; the Fédération Internationale de Football Association (or FIFA, its familiar abbreviation) for the world's most popular sport; and the Internet Corporation for Assigned Names and Numbers (also better known by its acronym, ICANN) for the Internet.

Yet, we have to do more than hope for serendipity resulting in solutions from the public-spiritedness of political leaders or the best from norm entrepreneurs, activists crossing borders, profit-seeking corporations, and transnational social networks. In accepting the limits of global governance without global government, our core argument is that numerous gaps should and could be filled in a variety of ways to address better the key problems confronting the world today. At the same time, these essential but mainly stop-gap measures should be taken without losing sight of the horizon and what may lie beyond. Vision is essential because history is not prophecy, nor are contemporary political constraints etched in stone. Yet, to do that we first need to rescue global governance from the temporal, spatial, and top-down strictures in which it is bound.

2

Why History Matters

Most things exist long before they have names. During one of his reflections about the sorry state of the interwar world, H. G. Wells used a description of the acceleration in transport and communication technologies, economic activity, and military reach to develop an argument about the need for a new form of political organization that was global in scale. His dramatic description was of a world struggling with change with the appearance of some initial inklings of what we would now call "globalization." But he was also portraying how these changes had brought with them alterations in the way that his world was governed.

Wells argued that only a world state could grab hold of those changes, harness them for good, and put an end to the wars that were – in his view – the outcome of an outmoded system of insufficient political delineation. As he put it, "a great part of our conflict [in the century before 1931] is due to [the] fact that almost all the governments of the world are too tight for the communities that they control." He continued: "If anybody had to plan sovereign governments for the world today you would never dream of divid-ing them up into such small areas."[1] His contention was that it was precisely because of this smallness of division that states would ultimately seek to expand, usually aggressively – as was proven a few short years later as fascist expansionism acted as a catalyst for the second fall into war in a generation.[2]

Wells was of course writing about a period that was far from unusual. Rapid change has been a feature of many historical moments and has precipitated as well as followed evolutions of and transformations in forms of global governance – as it has in our own day. This pattern was certainly true of the late eight-eenth and mid-nineteenth centuries in Europe and the effects of those changes on the parts of the world that Europeans sought to dominate; it was also visible in grand forms of political organiza-tion within and between large settled populations in South Asia, Southern Africa, East Asia, and Central and South America in ear-lier periods. What is distinctive about each epoch is the character of changes – in terms of their speed, content, and effect – and the systems of governance that they usher in and brush away. What is common – although the contents obviously are different – is that particular and sometimes unique ideas, institutions, rules, norms, and mechanisms shape world order at these moments in time.

The importance of what Wells had to say lies not so much in his comments about rapid change in the preceding century as in his observation that structures and institutions governing world order existed long before the term "global governance" was coined. His was an attempt to call for the active movement from one system to another. This realization unlocks the analytical utility of global governance, not only because it liberates the term from a tight association with the post-Cold War era but also – as we see in the

43

next chapter – because it disturbs the all too neat assumption that the "global" part of global governance must be planetary in scale.

Our task in this chapter is to continue to explore the ahistorical quality of thinking about global governance. Our purpose is to show why – and how – history matters when we examine the nuts and bolts that govern any world order. We begin by stepping back to revisit aspects of the genesis of the term "global governance," which we finessed earlier. We then refine the distinctions between what we term changes *in* (adaptations) versus changes *of* (transformations) the governance of world orders. We conclude by returning to our core themes to probe the drivers of continuity and change in global governance.

Stepping Back

We began by identifying the indelible mark left on the term "global governance" by the circumstances of its birth, the end of Cold War hostilities, and the collapse of the Soviet Union. We did so to wrest the term from the moment of its neological creation, to use it as a device to understand better the transformational components that have given rise to particular world orders past, present, and future as well as the drivers of those transformations through time. For us, global governance is not merely a descriptor for a post-Cold War pluralistic moment in which many actors rose to prominence on the world stage amid growing interdependence; it is also a legitimate set of questions about how the world is governed and ordered at all levels and in all historical periods. Conceptualized in this way, there has always been "global" governance, just not with the geographical dimensions that we now understand.

Importantly, we distinguish between global governance as a general phenomenon and its individual components and between changes of grand arrangements and more particular alterations within them; and we ask more detailed questions about when it began.

Understanding global governance as a general phenomenon (and the changes that it has undergone) requires tracing the mechanisms of the management of world order back in time. It also requires tracing epochs of global governance, with the distinctions between them marked by transitions and overlap. They need not be dramatic breaks with the past – indeed, they may result from the aggregation of many minor, frequently messy, seldom linear adjustments – but over time they nonetheless constitute clear departures from earlier systems of management and order worldwide. An improved understanding of this nature can enable us to determine how global governance could be altered to produce better outcomes, for humanity and for the planet.

To be clear, our purpose is not to provide a definitive history of global governance or to locate in time the precise point of its emergence. Rather, we aim to refashion the concept so that it has utility in explaining how world orders are fashioned and governed at particular moments as well as to understand transitions in, and transformations of, those arrangements. By presenting global governance as a structured inquiry into the construction and management of world order, we encourage others to go beyond the specific recent moment with which the term is associated. While global governance emerged, and was intimately associated, with post-Cold War efforts to realize the potential of the United Nations and the possibilities for an array of non-state actors, pertinent questions extend far beyond that instant. Yet, the association with a normative project to realize the UN's potential as imagined by its founders – whether working in concert with a range of other actors or not – and its use as a convenient label for what international organizations do, or could and should do, has frozen the term in time and thereby reduced its analytical utility. Everything that the UN system has done over the last three-quarters of a century has been a contribution to global governance; but global governance is far more than the activities in which the United Nations and other international organizations are engaged. Inquiries into the arrangements and management of world order should imbue global governance with a broader sensitivity to time – an understanding that the ideas, actors, institutions, and mechanisms that govern world order today are the outcome of departures from and evolutions in earlier systems of global governance.

As we have noted, too few scholars have been historically informed in their understanding of and engagement with global governance. Even among those who have, their focus has been on the modern history of international organization rather than the governance of world orders long past. As Craig Murphy puts it: "no social scientist or historian is yet able to give a credible account of global governance over . . . many millennia." Even less work has focused on possible future configurations of global governance, utopian or dystopian, with most analyses confined to thinking about the prospects for a world state or utopian and dystopian visions accompanied by science-fiction-like speculation.[3]

If we have overlooked or, at the least, been distracted from observing changes in the nature of power and authority within and across the world in the post-World War II era, we have been even less sensitive to the drivers of change and continuity, as well as their significance in moving from one world order to the next. We often use the language of *Pax Britannica* and *Pax Americana* as short-hand for world-order epochs and their transitions, but we seldom offer a compelling account of not only what changed between the two but also why and how. IR scholars are famously Eurocentric in their descriptions of world orders and the systems though which they are governed.[4] Lending the concept a capacity to understand better systems of governance back in time and on a far wider and more cosmopolitan scale (as in the next chapter) should allow us to begin a process to correct earlier standard operating procedures.

Organizing principles are a key but not the only part of solving this puzzle. What Murphy calls the "inter-Imperial World" of the nineteenth century – wherein European empires competed with one another over land, resources, power, and influence – was not organized simply through a compact by France, Austria, Prussia, Russia, and the United Kingdom. The Concert of Europe explained how that inter-imperial world was ordered to the extent that its management ensured that the European empires did not go to war with one another – that is, how it governed their coexistence. At the same time, there is little appreciation in the literature about the principles by which the rest of the world was organized – social Darwinism, racial segregation, and *mission civilisatrice* – and the mechanisms that served to subjugate non-white populations of the non-European world. We know that the "tutelage" – as Article 22 of the Covenant of the League of Nations put it – of "peoples not yet able to stand by themselves" lurks somewhere in the background of the dominant intellectual canon to justify colonization and its continuation. And we have underestimated the extent to which *terra nullius, terra incognita,* and other cartographic inscriptions also enabled the governance of the non-European world through conquest and acquisition.[5]

Among the grand ideas that informed the inter-imperial (and later the anti-imperial) system of global governance was certainly a blend of a wide variety of interests. We have yet to grasp, however, the specific expressions of organization that took concrete form based on these principles – the sources of power and forms of authority that they established, generated, and entrenched as well as their consequences. We are undoubtedly closer to understanding the forms of governing the world that resulted from the newer ordering principles of US hegemony; we are nevertheless still far removed from mastering them completely. These principles – self-determination and economic liberalization, to name the most prominent – blended progress with self-interest. Self-determination opened the opportunity for colonized peoples to govern themselves and for US commercial interests to have access to previously closed colonial markets. Economic liberalization was both a commitment to a free flow of goods worldwide and a selectively applied program that fell short of opening up key sectors to external competition (of which agriculture is still perhaps the most significant). These principles gave rise to forms of formal and informal organization that have since shaped the world around us; and they have changed and mutated over time. They have also left legacies that continue to affect the daily lives of many of the world's most precariously placed populations, with arbitrary borders and asymmetrical systems of trade being among the most prominent.[6]

An essential missing element is the how and why of moving from the inter-imperial world to *Pax Americana*. The Quaker economist Kenneth Boulding often quipped: "We are where we are because we got there." Yet, truly to comprehend how we have arrived at contemporary forms of order – as many are continuations of, or responses to, previous incarnations – we need to understand how global governance, before it was so labelled, was manifest and altered over time. We also need to understand how competing forms coexisted rather than simply to accept what is around us and try to understand its abstraction from historical developments. This lacuna is important when considering not only the competing forms of global governance that the Cold War facilitated, or the harrowing counterfactuals that a Nazi-dominated system would have generated, but also how older forms of world order were born and passed away. Only then can we understand how and why we got to where we are, as well as where we could go from here.

It becomes clearer that we must have something to offer if we turn our attention to the big questions of global governance. The data clearly show that those countries that were the richest in 1820 have, in large measure, prospered the most since (more often than not, dramatically so), not just in crude measures such as per capita income but also in health and other social indicators. We also know that it is from this period that the organizational forms that we recognize today as international institutions were nascent, taking off with gusto from the 1850s – although, to reiterate, we should be careful not to confuse "international institutions" with "global governance," because the former are merely one specific, historically contingent element of the latter. Complex forms of command and control facilitated the consolidation of European and later US power, and the opportunities enabled by these systems partially explain the dramatic and growing prosperity of those countries that were already doing well at the outset of the nineteenth century. Yet, almost no one – in IR at least – has sought to demonstrate how various periods of global governance and world order have contributed to the accumulation of wealth for some and the relative and absolute impoverishment of others.[7]

In extending such questions backwards in time, we can realize how forms of organization contributed to the success and demise of particular regimes and civilizations, which in turn can contribute to our knowledge about how best, and how best not, to struggle and improve the governance of the contemporary world. The examination of how some orders mutated – such as the morphing of the Roman Empire into the Holy Roman Empire or the Holy See into today's papacy – could shed light on the forms of governance and principles of organization that generated greater propensities to peace, war, growth, or atrophy. Ancient Rome and ancient China are useful examples in terms of the perceived differences between the two empires and the similarities in their internal and external forms of governance and domination as well as their demise.[8] Moreover, there are interesting questions of transition between mergers of and relationships among imperial systems that could help us better understand the governance of the classical and not so classical worlds. They are part of the alloy that has helped temper today's world order.

Equally, the mechanisms that governed empires – the various forms of administration, organization, and management – can tell us much about elements of contemporary political contestation as well as about the forms of order and disorder that we almost had and thus should seek to avoid. The use of islands by the British imperial authorities as prisons, places of forced exile, and spaces to be emptied for colonial need is an example of a form of colonial governance that continues to reverberate and have everyday implications.[9] Another example is the construction of an impenetrable hedge and heavily guarded customs line of some 3,700 kilometers that stretched between the Indus and the Mahanadi rivers to ensure that salt taxes were collected across India during the colonial period. Yet another example is the historic and contemporary building of walls and other physical barriers to discipline, disrupt, separate, and contain particular populations.[10] Such technologies of governing played a crucial role in shaping daily life and the health experiences of many during the nineteenth century.[11] The tributary systems attempted by Nazi Germany and Imperial Japan during the 1930s and 1940s were forms of interstate organization that stand out as prominent illustrations of precisely the kinds of vision and experiments that we should seek to avoid.[12] Writing in the 1930s, the British social historian Ralph Fox stated that "the existence of the Empire exercises a decisive influence on the life, and very often also the death, of every British-born man or woman."[13] Clearly, empire had a dramatic impact on the lives of colonial subjects too. Investigating how this and other forms of organization – the worthy as well as the "to be avoided" – affect and have affected ordinary lives is a key motivation for understanding better previous types of global governance. This perspective animates the penultimate chapter of this book.

Thus, understanding how the world is organized and governed is a prerequisite for building a better foundation for where we should – and thus could – be headed. Nonetheless, a plan for a better world is conspicuous by its absence. Instead of a grand debate about how to make the world fairer and more habitable, at best we formulate policies to muddle through and at worst justify ingenious ways to show that dramatic change is unfeasible. We do ourselves, the field, and the planet no service by removing from our job descriptions the need to put forward and actively debate alternative visions of more desirable world orders. We should thus be clear about our ultimate objectives.

Part of the problem is that we lack an appreciation for what drives change in the way that our world is organized, which leaves our intellectual undertaking as ahistorical as, for instance, contemporary mainstream economics,[14] a discipline once linked but now largely disconnected from the intellectual industry of historians. Economics is, of course, far from alone in eschewing history. Andrew Hurrell has chided IR scholars for their affection for and affliction with "relentless presentism."[15] "History" might be something that we introduce to students in the opening lectures of an introductory class about IO and global governance. However, we tend to treat history as an empirical treasure trove in which we can find examples that fit, or can be made to fit, the way that we choose to explain forms of world organization; or, alternatively, we concentrate narrowly on concepts or particular issues, which in turn obscure striking lessons gleaned from studying historical developments. We seldom reach back further than the establishment of the UN system, albeit sometimes accompanied by fleeting references to the League of Nations and the nineteenth-century public unions. Looking for the drivers of growth, a concern with how the world is governed, and how this governance has changed over time could help us better understand the forms of organization that have contributed to the prosperity enjoyed by some states and the poverty suffered by the vast majority of others.

We have cited Craig Murphy's 1994 *International Organization and Industrial Change* because it illuminates the role played by international organizations as modes of governance in advancing forms of economic accumulation. His work with JoAnne Yates on what we have elsewhere called "creeping" global governance[16] shows how minute, functionalist developments that standardize economic behavior and social norms lock in place systems of command and control that in turn give rise to particular economic outcomes and social goods (some beneficial, some not). They are notable exceptions in a field that has consistently underperformed in accounting for change, particularly in systems of global governance. Even this ray of light, however, is obscured and enables us to peer back only into the relatively recent past rather than into epochs long ago. If global governance is to be a legitimate analytical tool, it must explain change not just today or in and between the post-Cold War and inter-imperial eras but also in other times and under different circumstances.

Differentiating Changes *in* from Changes *of* Global Governance

It is worth dwelling a little longer on exactly how one might identify what constitutes changes *in* global governance – that is, adjustments *in* a system – as distinct from more substantial changes *of* global governance – that is, fundamental transformations *of* a system. This distinction is particularly important because periods of transition, both in and of global governance, can be marked by extended periods of ambiguity and uncertainty.

It is useful at this point to spell out what we consider are markers of change in the recent history of global governance so that we are better able to move back in time, as well as forwards, to understand when change has happened, what kind of change it was, and how it was brought about. To do this, we begin by looking backwards from the current moment to identify possible markers of transition, when the previous system was under duress and ending, and contemporary global governance underage and emerging. It is also important to make clear that transitions are necessarily messy; they make generalizations hazardous. Clean breaks from one system to another rarely occur, with residues and echoes of previous systems enduring as lasting features of earlier formations.

It is useful to recall in this respect, as Robert Jackson reminded us, that even the Peace of Westphalia – a foundation stone of current IR theory and practice – was not so much an abrupt break between two eras as an important indication of the emergence of a new European order of sovereign states that overshadowed imperial and papal and other religious authorities.[17] It was not until the advent of decolonization over three centuries later, however, that sovereignty actually emerged across the globe as the universal principle of authority. Moreover, the declaration of its demise has also been premature – "bringing the state back in"[18] was a catchy title from three analysts in the 1980s but was inaccurate because the state never left. Susan Strange's catchy title "the retreat of the state" was less compelling than her subtitle "the diffusion of power in the world economy,"[19] which more recently was depicted by Tana Johnson as "organizational progeny."[20]

Five questions help us move toward being better positioned to draw distinctions between systems of global governance as well as to detect changes within them:

1 What are the overarching organizational principles and ideologies and the underpinning relations of power?
2 How do rules at all levels of human activity relate to principles, ideologies, and power?

3 Which actors, institutions, and mechanisms are involved in the organization and governance of a world order?

4 How are they arranged?

5 What are the consequences of organizing and governing the world in this fashion?

The answers to these questions enable us to distinguish clearly between the eighteenth- and nineteenth-century systems of global governance and the one consolidated after 1945. We summarize quickly here the developments that form the basis for continued discussions when applied to space in the next chapter. They also permit us to identify the period from the onset of World War I to the end of World War II as a period of upheaval and transition in which hostilities were far from settled and global configurations of power (in particular the remaining European empires and subjugated peoples) unresolved.[21] During the eighteenth and nineteenth centuries, the shifting relations of power among the European imperial countries provided the foundations for world order. Relations between the main European powers and other states were governed by war and formal institutions – such as the Holy Alliance and the Concert of Europe already mentioned – as well as complex systems of diplomatic exchanges, with the type and extent of those interactions determining the status and significance of each state at any given moment.[22]

Complex diplomatic mores were not, however, the only means governing the nineteenth-century world order. Also at play were ideas about and mechanisms of racial hierarchy, imperial entitlement, unequal commerce, and military might. Indeed, to focus on diplomatic systems alone would signify that the governance of that world order was simply about the European world and relations between the dominant states therein. Moreover, other complex and extensive characteristics governed nineteenth-century world order. Military occupations and proxy regimes combined to subjugate non-white populations and colonize lands, often in concert with private actors and in collaboration with local elites. Systems of colonial governance were exploitative by their very nature and designed to extract maximum value for the metropole from the periphery. Complex forms of emerging global governance were manifest in the programs of industrial, commercial, and telecommunications standard-setting. These activities acted as catalysts for the development of international public unions. Conference diplomacy emerged to tackle those pressing problems of the day that were a blight on the imperial systems. The growth of international law that concretized land and commercial property rights, along with the growth of philanthropic actors enabled by the accumulation of wealth from industrialization, reinforced relations of power underpinning world order.[23] These systems were made possible by earlier processes of resource and wealth extraction – including, but not limited to, the trade in and trafficking of humans across the globe – that had given the European states elevated positions from which to consolidate their power.

The rise of the United States as the pre-eminent world power coupled with the demise of European imperial systems eventually ushered in a new era. Yet, the interwar period as the era of transition also saw elements of the old system persevere. They were manifest in attempts to continue the *ancien régime* through an institutional structure aspiring to universal membership in the form of the League of Nations. However, the weakness in the underlying arrangement of power at that time, along with growing but not yet consolidated pre-eminence of the United States, ushered in an interregnum between systems that ended only with the termination of World War II. The new system – the onset of the one in which we reside today – put in place new structures and ways of operating, which drew upon new constellations of actors and operated according to different principles and ideologies. One such innovation was the shift from complex diplomatic mores and exchanges as the means by which interactions among the "great" powers were ordered to a form of system management through "club diplomacy" in multilateral institutions.

In its immediate incarnation, two competing blocs, each with ideologically and militarily dominant states (the Soviet Union and the United States, respectively) governed the order. A commitment to self-determination as an organizing principle eliminated or weakened most of the remaining vestiges of European imperialism. However, with the end of the Cold War and the eventual collapse of the Soviet Union, global governance shifted to a system centered primarily on US power. The forms of diplomacy, international legal apparatuses, and modes of operation that Washington favored and the alliances upon which it relied for its military might were reinforced by a host of non-state actors that mainly favored the status quo. Complex political and economic institutions and mechanisms evolved to cement this system: international commercial law; transnational governance institutions; regulatory and accountability actors and mechanisms; firms; NGOs; philanthropic institutions; and private military and security companies, among many others. Market actors and innovations nurtured increasingly standardized forms of economic behavior – albeit with notable local and regional variations. The growth of large-scale media and social-media providers and actors has consolidated the system further.

Notable challenges to US power have subsequently arisen, but they have disrupted rather than supplanted that hegemony. While the Trump administration undermines the rules-based order that the United States created and championed, some of the most significant challengers – notably China but including other emerging powers as well – have tended to engage in system-preserving rather than status quo-transforming behavior, although the rhetoric is often distinct.[24] While tensions with other challengers are noteworthy, such as with the Russian Federation in Syria and Ukraine, US exceptionalism persists but is tolerated for the time being. That reality is manifest in the Trump administration's withdrawal from the UN Educational, Scientific and Cultural Organization (UNESCO); its exit from the UN Human Rights Council; its total cut in funding for the UN Population Fund; its departure from the Paris Climate Agreement; its refusal to allow the appointment of WTO appellate body members for fear that rulings may go against US interests; a stated ambition to renegotiate the North American Free Trade Agreement (NAFTA) after withdrawing from the Trans-Pacific Partnership, along with *ad hoc* tariffs and other restrictive trade measures; the dramatic escalation of tension with North Korea that preceded the June 2018 Singapore summit between Donald Trump and Kim Jong-un; and Trump's tantrums at the G7 and NATO summits in the summer of 2018 as preparations for his embrace of Russia's authoritarian Vladimir Putin.

What we are able to see are clear differences between the systems of global governance in place today and those that ordered the world in the first half of the twentieth century and earlier in the inter-imperial era. In so doing, we glimpse how we can detect what drives change as well as what triggers adjustments. We are also able to see that suggestions about the death or even the imminent demise of the current system are premature. For it even to be on the wane, the answers to our five questions about today's world order would have to be very different from what they are at present. While elements would endure – as they have from previous systems – in order to signal a significant change there would need to be many more indications of substantial movements in the relations of power and dominant organizational principles and ideologies. The systems of rules that organize human activity at every level would likely be distinctly different. The same would also be true for the actors, institutions, and mechanisms involved in the governance of world order as they would be for the outcomes produced.

Conclusion: Prisoner of the Present, Continuity, or Change?

Francis Fukuyama trumpeted "the end of history" at the outset of the post-Cold War era.[25] He was wrong then, as would anyone else have been at any time who argued the same. This chapter's premise is quite the opposite, namely that deep historical familiarity is necessary to interpret systems of world-order management today and tomorrow as well as yesterday.

It is thus worth circling back to our claim at the outset that we would seek to attenuate confusion by reclaiming global governance's unrealized analytical utility and by rescuing its normative potential. Our point of departure was that we must move from a simple association with the actions and activities of international organizations and their subsidiaries along with those of non-state actors to questions that probe the intricate and multifaceted manner that the world is governed and ordered at any given moment in time. The introduction of historical linkages to elements of today's world order is an essential part of the effort to generate better understandings of the complex elements that combine to produce distinctive world orders and that enable us to see how the world has been, is, and will be governed. In particular, our plea to liberate ourselves from the limited time period of the post-Cold War moment is an initial attempt to interpret the varying systems of global governance that have existed over the ages.

After pushing out the perspectives on time, we are now ready to apply a parallel effort to rethink the spatial limitations that typically constrain our efforts to conceptualize *global* governance. We need to comprehend the forces that have driven and continue to drive continuity and change and that propel stability and transformation, as well as the overlap and ambiguity in previous world orders that have been less than worldwide but which have nonetheless governed substantial parts of the globe and left a legacy of ideas, norms, practices, procedures, and institutions.

3

Planetary Isn't the Point

In the final pages of *Waiting for the Barbarians,* J. M. Coetzee's unnamed magistrate reflects on the frameworks of understanding forced upon the inhabitants of lands outside of the "Empire" - their supposed savagery, incivility, and ever-present threat. He laments "I wanted to live outside of the history that Empire imposes on its subjects, even its lost subjects. I never wished it for the barbarians that they should have the history of Empire laid upon them."[1]

There are lessons here for the way that we think about global governance. These are lessons about the dangers of reifying our understanding and failing to challenge existing conceptions. Our tradition is to understand global governance as we first named and encountered it. We have seldom looked beyond these first impressions to understand how the world is governed and ordered in all of its complexity - that is, beyond its intergovernmental core - or to grasp how it is manifest at different moments in time. The result is that we have restricted our capacity to comprehend other systems of order and control or to recognize them as instances of global governance. Moreover, because our understanding is bound up with the aspirations of the immediate post-Cold War era, we have been unable to see less attractive and pernicious systems as expressions of global governance. We have been, to put it succinctly, willing to see global governance as multilateralism but not as world government, world empire, or anything else.[2] The result has been to freeze our understanding in time, in space, and in aspiration. The effect has been the imposition of one conception of global governance on the history of world orders in a way that blinds us from comprehending their forms, effects, and internal constitutions in other eras – just as the "Empire" does in Coetzee's tale.

In this and the following chapter we take forward our claim that, in order to lend global governance the analytical traction required to rescue it from the particular moment of its linguistic appearance, we need to understand that as a phenomenon it has existed in eras before our own. We do so with the key qualifier that global governance will inevitably be manifest in qualitatively different ways at different moments in time. Thus, we should not seek to understand the global governance of eras gone by in the same way that we understand its manifestation in our own. Instead, we should – as Coetzee's magistrate would likely implore – set historical and future forms of global governance within the context of their own time and seek to understand them thus.

This chapter makes a key companion argument to that developed in the previous chapter: just as we sought to wrest our understanding of global governance from the grip of presentism, we need also to rescue it from an association with the planet as a distinguishing spatial and conceptual element. We do this because investigating the manner in which systems combine to organize, manage, govern, and arrange the world does not demand that those arrangements be planetary in scale. Indeed, in all eras before our own, the forms of global governance have been less than planetary in their reach and scale. The reconceptualization simply requires that they curate a good proportion of human-centered activity over large swathes of the world.

Our argument is motivated by two observations that we believe act to inhibit this aspect of global governance's analytical traction. The first is that existing conceptualizations invariably treat "global" synonymously with the planet. The second observation is that there exists a lack of familiarity – or perhaps even a reticence – with what the governance of world order might look like if it is not planetary in the same sense as our own: that is, if it is not, to paraphrase Coetzee, of the "Empire."

As is evident from the brief engagements with historical examples that we have introduced throughout this book, not all world orders have been global. This is as true for the nineteenth-century inter-imperial order as it is for uneasy arrangements among competing empires in the ancient world. In these and many other cases, the systems of order that orchestrated actions for a large share of humanity were not planetary in coverage or extent – though humanity at the time may well have imagined that they were. They were world orders nonetheless; we can identify the systems that lent order to those epochs as forms of global governance that require understanding. As we have observed, what is different about today's world order is that it is genuinely planetary in scale; we exist in the first epoch in which such an arrangement is possible.

That said, just because we have reached a moment when we can talk of planetary governance does not mean that all future constellations will necessarily be manifest in the same way – they could be smaller or more extensive. Although ongoing advances in technology and communications may lead us in that direction, moments of retreating global governance have also been evident in times gone by, as they were during the interwar years. A global scale is a distinguishing characteristic of our own epoch, and it may or may not be of others as well.

It is important to note, however, that areas of the globe need not be formally governed to be elements of a worldwide system of governance. Just as in the case of Coetzee's "barbarians," they can also take a position in opposition to, or be (consciously or otherwise) different or excluded from, a dominant system. What is key to our understanding is that such stances are taken in direct response to – and thus inevitably entail a measure of orientation around – a dominant system of world order.

Conceptualizing global governance in this way has considerable utility. It enables us to ask questions about the spatial and substantive constitution of different (and sometimes competing) systems of world-order management as well as of how areas outside of formally orchestrated space relate to relationships of command and control. This has particular pertinence when we think about the evolution of our own order. For example, at its inception, *Pax Americana* was far from global in reach and occupied a space also inhabited by declining empires and a nascent communist system. Later, during the Cold War, it coexisted alongside a competing Soviet-centered world order. Both of these orders not only organized life within their respective spheres of influence they also affected those areas that formally lay beyond but which were nonetheless oriented in relation to the Cold War's dominant powers – such as in those countries that considered themselves to be non-aligned and were members of the Non-Aligned Movement (NAM) or the Group of 77 (G77). Across this period, none of the world orders or their systems of management could genuinely be described as "global." They were, nevertheless, forms of global governance, and we should conceptualize and understand them as such.

Thus, our claim is that emphasizing history alone would be insufficient for understanding the whole of the global governance puzzle. To help solve it we also need to understand what space – real and imagined – means for global governance. Conceiving of global governance in this way enables us to ask questions about how non-planetary world orders were and are organized as well as how regulatory systems among small settlements governing relations among themselves at the outset of human evolution have developed into systems that define and determine the Anthropocene.

To support our claims, we explore the spatial evolution of one aspect of our own system of global governance. We do this by focusing on aspects of those institutions that have evolved with the greatest geographical reach to orchestrate aspects of contemporary global life. Many are intergovernmental, such as the formal organizations and institutional arrangements that attempt to regulate international trade and financial flows, respond to development challenges, promote peace and security, and alleviate humanitarian and environment crises. Others are private (such as financial institutions and the markets in which they and other economic actors participate), not for profit (for example, the Women's Environment and Development Organization, BRAC, and Amnesty International), faith-based (Christian Aid and Islamic Relief), and nefarious (terrorist, criminal, and mercenary groups). All have reaches and mandates that have evolved over time (positively and negatively) and that in many cases have made them more global; moreover, their actions and activities – and those of many others – combine to govern our world order.

The focus here is on state-based institutions because their evolution illustrates well the spatial expansion of global governance over time. We are, nonetheless, mindful that this perspective provides only one slice of the current system's creation story and is thus incomplete. A more elaborate picture would also take in the evolution of global financial actors and markets, aid and relief NGOs, faith-based actors, and criminal networks and terrorist groups, among many others.

In pursuit of our aims, the rest of the chapter unfolds as follows. It begins by parsing our use of the term "global." Here we raise questions about the need to define strictly the term as a system of order on a planetary scale. The chapter then explores a little of the evolution of the main intergovernmental elements of our own world order – starting well before the term "global governance" was coined – paying attention to the changing realities and the characteristics of the planet as well as conceptions of space therein. Throughout we show how, despite important institutional advances, these elements helped orchestrate world order on a less than planetary scale until we reach the current era. We suggest why the rubric of *global* governance is appropriate nonetheless.

The Meaning of "Global"

In common parlance, "global" is an adjective that applies to everything happening in every corner of the world. Our challenge is to push back against this tendency toward totality and to rethink differences in scale in a geographic sense in order to adapt analytically the "global" in global governance so that it does not signify "planetary" as a literal interpretation would require. We do this to enable the word "global" to capture the sum of the human forces governing world order at any specific moment in time. Thus, we also seek to transcend the "international" in the common association between global governance and what international organizations do, to move toward an understanding of the governance of world orders over time, which may or may not include international organizations. Along with the distortions that arise from unwisely restricting understandings of the dynamics of global governance to the post-Cold War moment, the meaning of "global" as "planetary" unnecessarily deprives global governance of analytical purchase for posing essential and even existential questions in the analysis of earlier epochs.

It is also worth noting that we apply "global" in another sense. Rather than a realm of international governance – which better describes what states do in international organizations and institutional arrangements – we follow common convention in also deploying "global" as a wider net within which we are able to capture a range of actors, institutions, and mechanisms. Thus, when we talk about global governance we mean both the sum of the activities orchestrating human relations and the broadest range of actors, institutions, and mechanisms involved therein. As noted, while it might be the case that ours is the first era to have ideas, institutions, technologies, and material capabilities that genuinely touch every corner of the world, both of these usages of the term are applicable across other times and different understandings of space.

In part, we are taking a clue from "world history," which argues that events within particular societies must be viewed in context and as part of what was taking place across a wider geographical landscape. *World* historians look through wide spatial lenses; but they do not necessarily take the entire "world" as their unit of analysis or feel obliged to incorporate events in every corner in order to hazard generalizations.[3] For instance, J. R. McNeill and William H. McNeill provide "a bird's-eye view of world history" over the last 6,000 years by examining a series of "webs,"[4] even though many of those webs cover only a small proportion of the Earth's territory. Thus, while in the Anthropocene it seems logical to speak of global governance as planetary governance, this does not mean that the term's analytical pertinence is reduced when applied to earlier times. Rather, it suggests merely that the range of geographical and conceptual coverage was less encompassing.

Freeing global governance spatially as well as temporally allows a more dynamic understanding of how systems of world order evolve and endure. One part of understanding the story of the evolution of our own era of global governance lies in appreciating how European imperialisms and missions of conquest evolved and, earlier, how the Roman Empire bled into the Holy Roman Empire. Additional pieces of our puzzle are to be found in examining and explaining how transitions took place in Africa (such as the Kingdom of Zimbabwe and the Empire of Mali); the Middle East (for instance, the Ottoman Empire and the Khedivate of Egypt); Asia (for example, the Mongol Empire of Genghis Khan and the Han Dynasty of China); and Latin America (as with the Aztec, Inca, Mayan, and Olmec empires). We now turn to understanding the spatial evolution of one part of the more recent aspects of our own system to illustrate the salience of our proposed approach.

Foundations of Contemporary Global Governance

One starting point for thinking about the geographical scale of previous expressions of global governance and their spatial expansion is to consider the size and growth of the human population over time, the forms of political settlement into which humanity was organized, and the mechanisms of governance that existed among and between these units. Our aim is not to retell world history from its beginnings but instead to pick a point in time from which we explore a little of the immediate evolution of our own system of global governance – elements of which we have also explored elsewhere in this book – and track its subsequent spatial expansion through time. The point of our choosing is the early nineteenth century, a moment when some of the features of contemporary global governance had begun to emerge and augment as well as to challenge pillars of the existing system.

Our choice, however, comes with a significant health warning. In exploring a little of its spatial expansion from 1800 onwards, we risk closely associating global governance with European – and, later, US – orchestrated world orders. We do not wish this mistake to be made. For the sake of argument, and because of the limits of space, we do not trace global governance further back in time to account for, say, the fourteenth-century expansion of the Timurid Empire into the Middle East, Russia, and Eastern Europe, the system of control that it put into place, or the management of relations with littoral and more distant empires; nor do we set out to elaborate on the governance of world orders at the time of the Han, Parthian, or Roman empires. Rather, our purpose is to explore the beginnings of our own system for the purposes of illustrating our argument that "planetary isn't the point."

At the outset of the nineteenth century, the population of the planet was approximately 1 billion. Continuing a pattern of habitation that had remained relatively consistent since at least the second century CE, most of this population was distributed north of the equator in a flat arc from Europe (20.8 percent) to South and East Asia (64.9 percent combined, with modern-day India and China comprising the lion's share) – with Africa, the Americas, and Oceania comprising 10.9, 3.2, and 0.2 percent respectively. Politically, the world was organized into a bricolage of states, kingdoms, sultanates, principalities, electorates, city-states, emirates, empires, khanates, prince-bishoprics, shōgunates, landgraviates, margraviates, duchies, archduchies, nations, monarchies, imamates, republics, and confederacies. Yet, for all this political diversity, it was European imperial power that was the dominate mode of governance. The British, Danish, Dutch, French, Portuguese, Ottoman, Russian, Spanish, and Swedish empires formally governed much of the early nineteenth-century world and informally orchestrated even more.

The years running up to 1800 had been times of considerable change – in industry, agriculture, and communications and transportation technologies, among many others. The turn of the nineteenth century was also a period of significant political flux and transition, both within and between states, as it was an age of war. As Eric Hobsbawm put it,

> From 1792 until 1815 there was almost uninterrupted war in Europe, combined or coincident with occasional war outside: in the West Indies, the Levant and India in the 1790s and early 1800s,

in occasional naval operations abroad thereafter, in the USA in 1812–14. The consequences of victory or defeat in these wars were considerable, for they transformed the map of the world.[5]

Other key challenges of the early 1800s included health (smallpox, syphilis, flu, cholera, and typhus, among others) and natural disasters, as well as those problems thrown up by early-stage industrialization and the spread of communications technologies. It was these challenges and others that helped drive the emergence of transnational and international institutions and accompanying systems of rules and norms of behavior. The Concert of Europe sought to preserve peaceable relations among the European powers while enabling them to continue to pursue their accumulation of colonial possessions in the non-European world. International public unions facilitated the smooth flow of communications. Conference diplomacy mushroomed to address issues of health, welfare, and morality. Standard-setting began in earnest to harmonize everything from railroad gauges to postal systems and rights and duties in international commerce. A blend of soft and hard power, alliances (often shifting) with state and non-state actors, and diplomatic mores enabled the European powers to govern near and distant lands.

Over the course of the following century, this system of governance steadily grew to encompass a greater proportion of humanity and geographic space. Formal and informal conquest resulted in new colonies. The diversity of political units that had characterized the turn of the nineteenth century shifted considerably, with many combining to form states, while others were consumed in the expansion and contraction of empires. Participation in international conferences and public unions grew. Increased trade and the spread of communications technologies harmonized practices and brought greater interdependence. The result was to extend – both geographically and substantively – the inter-imperial system of global governance further across humanity and the planet.

By 1900, the relations of power underpinning this system and its institutions had shifted again, as had the ideas that legitimized its rule. German industrialization and unification, and Germany's acquisition of colonies in Africa and the Pacific, challenged the European inter-imperial order from within;[6] the rise of the United States in the post-revolution and post-civil war periods challenged it from outside.[7] These changes had a profound effect on the shape of global governance as well as its spatial expansion. Many more of the world's now 1.65 billion population became entangled in the machineries of governance. This expansion included not only the growth in populations in existing colonial states but also new areas that were brought under formal control – most notably in Asia and Africa.

Yet, it was not just hard power that drove this system's expansion. Technological and industrial innovation played a role not only in driving advances in production and communication but also in assisting the formal colonization of a greater proportion of the world's population and landmass by the European powers. Lending legitimacy to this expansion were ideas of racial superiority, and the driving interests were to be found in resource acquisition and market expansion. The empires of six European countries led this colonial charge – Belgium, the Netherlands, France, Portugal, Spain, and the United Kingdom.

However, the high tide of European imperialism ebbed as the twentieth century dawned and the relations of power underpinning this system of global governance had already begun to break down. By 1914, this breakdown had become a collapse, and Europe went to war. While much of the conflict was played out on the continent itself, the extent of the nineteenth-century imperial systems and the alliances that had preceded the outbreak of war ensured that large parts of the globe were involved in what became the first "world" war. And while World War I may not have been truly "global" in a planetary sense, the sheer scale of the systems of governance in place nevertheless entangled – in one way or another – a significant proportion of humanity.

The impact of the war outside of Europe varied dramatically – from simple declarations of support for one side or another to the supply of significant numbers of troops and involvement in the armed conflict itself. Its history was one that was nevertheless written predominantly as a European affair, and not one that involved many millions from East and South Asia, Australasia, Africa, and the Middle East or which did not end neatly in parts of the world with the 11 November 1918 Armistice.[8] It nevertheless disrupted the established system of global governance and precipitated, among many other things, the collapse of the Russian, Austro-Hungarian, and Ottoman empires, the weakening of British and French power, and the rise of the United States. Indeed, such was the rupture in the relations of global power that the war began a transitional phase from one system of global governance to another.

First Try at World Organization

While the foundations of some of today's international organizations can be traced back to these nineteenth- and early twentieth-century happenings, they are better anchored in the process of institutionalization that took place after World War I and the shifting locus of power from the eastern to the western Atlantic which precipitated that process. Here we find the origins of many of the international institutions that, today, are mainstays – but not the only aspects – of the global governance that we currently know. It is also in this transitional moment that we see new ideas emerging to challenge existing thinking, older ones enduring, new material capabilities sitting alongside diminishing capacity, technological advances abutting traditional machineries, new and old systems of rules and actors continuing side by side, and newly forged alliances accompanying novel as well as persistent behavior. These and myriad other elements of continuity and change combined to create an alloy out of which the post-World War II system of global governance was forged but which began in the aftermath of World War I and the 1919 Paris Peace Accords.

It is worth noting a few of the sharper features of the period to remind ourselves of the forces at play during this era of transition. Somewhere between 17 and 18 million combatants and civilians were killed during World War I and a further 23 million wounded. Another 50 million were killed in 1918 by a flu epidemic thought to have points of origin in China and military camps in France and the United States. The global ideological landscape continued to change with anti-imperial ideas proliferating alongside communist, anarchist, fascist, and social Darwinist visions. Norman Stone remarked of the period:

> At the end of the First World War, men and women saw that the era of European predominance was coming to an end. There was socialism at home, a threat to the old order; there was Bolshevism

abroad. America – aggressively democratic – dominated the world's economy, though not as firmly as in the late 1940s. There were colonial revolts, of which no one could foresee the outcome, and a "Third-World" country, Japan, had shown Europe how she might be defeated.[9]

It is against this backdrop that the victors sought to create an organization to promote peace and security – the League of Nations – which was intended to be the first genuinely universal organization, with all states represented, and which would abate violence- and war-generating tendencies. Comprising an assembly, a council, an administrative secretariat, and the Permanent Court of International Justice, its architecture established an organizational form that would eventually be carried forward after World War II – albeit in a modified form[10] – in the United Nations.

Forty-eight countries attended the first Assembly of the League of Nations in December 1920; a total of sixty-three countries joined the organization between 1920 and 1946. However, state participation in, and membership of, the League was marked by absence and instability. At its greatest extent it counted fifty-eight members; but this number lasted for only the five months between September 1934 and February 1935. The United States chose not to join the League despite the efforts by US president Woodrow Wilson leading to its creation. Of the forty-two founding members, only twenty-three remained for the duration of the organization's existence. Most withdrew, others were annexed – Albania and Ethiopia by Italy, and Austria and Czechoslovakia by Nazi Germany[11] – and the Soviet Union was expelled.

Nonetheless, the League was an organization that attempted to bring a measure of order on a scale that had not been known or attempted before. Moreover, the spatial reach of this new system of global governance was furthered through the handing over of control of German and Ottoman colonies to the victorious powers under the League's mandate and protectorates system. Though intended to be arrangements of stewardship, these provisions inevitably enabled the victors of World War I to augment their own influence. Under the mandate system, the United Kingdom presided over Palestine, Tanganyika, British Cameroons, British Togoland, and Mesopotamia. France was entrusted with Syria, French Cameroun, and French Togoland. The Free City of Danzig, Saarland, and Memel Territory were placed under the direct control of the League of Nations. Belgium was entrusted with Ruanda-Urundi. Japan administered the South Pacific Mandate. And complicated co-stewardship arrangements existed for the Territory of New Guinea (Australia and the United Kingdom), Nauru (Australia, New Zealand, and the United Kingdom), and South West Africa (the Republic of South Africa and the United Kingdom).

Alongside the League of Nations, a range of other institutions addressed specific problems and issues. Most notable among these was the International Labour Organization (ILO), although the Health Organization and the International Commission on Intellectual Cooperation were also important. The ILO aimed to dissipate social unrest through enhancing the rights of workers worldwide in an effort to abate further Bolshevik-style revolutions challenging the authority of Western ruling elites.[12] Taken together, these organizations provided some of the institutional foundations upon which observers hoped world peace could be built.

However, the League of Nations proved to be unsuccessful.

While it survived in name until 1946, when the remainder of its activities and its real estate were transferred to its successor, it was hampered throughout its existence by the self-interested tendencies of the European powers, the shortcomings of its Covenant, the failure of the United States to participate, and the handling of Germany's defeat.[13] Hans. J. Morgenthau argued that "The inability of the League of Nations to maintain international order and peace . . . was the inevitable result of the ascendancy that the ethics and policies of sovereign nations were able to maintain over the moral and political objectives of . . . international government."[14] The League of Nations was, of course, not intended to be a world government any more than the United Nations. Both were born of conviction and experience and a pragmatism to alter fundamentally the way that states conducted their affairs. The League was, nonetheless, an early attempt to harness state power for the management of problems – many of which have since become even more acute and certainly more global.

Inevitably, the League's reputation and authority were tarnished by its shortcomings as well as dramatic failures in Manchuria and Ethiopia, among others. Yet, in the economic and social arena, it succeeded in largely unheralded ways in doing useful work. As Patrick Cottrell puts it, from the ashes of the League arose a

cognitive blueprint . . . that represented a major leap forward in the realm of functional cooperation and the promotion of human rights . . . [The] League secretariat and spinoff organizations provided the human capacity to manage many different international problems from technical areas such as broadcasting to humanitarian issues such as health and refugees . . . [And its] economic and financial apparatus provided a valuable stabilizing function during the interwar years and laid the groundwork for the post-World War II liberal economic order.[15]

Recent research has also indicated the extent to which the League's mandate system – despite the intentions of the European colonial powers – laid the groundwork for anti-imperial reactions and the decolonization that began and then accelerated far more quickly than imagined after World War II.[16] Indeed, those initial rumblings continue in modern political geography, which began when World War I resulted in the disintegration of four empires and sounded the death knell for the others.

The League of Nations also conducted research and formulated policies that were successful in curbing inflation in Austria, Hungary, and elsewhere in the early 1920s. It proposed economic policies based on open trade. And it discussed the mounting employment problem of the 1920s and 1930s in a clear and "modern" manner. One might argue that, for subsequent development, there was too much focus on the economic shortcomings of the Great Depression and their impact on the industrialized countries of Europe and North America. There was thus too little attention to – or even awareness of – the weaknesses and failures of development in the rest of the world, most of which (with the exception of Latin America) remained under colonial domination.

The economic and political gales faced by the League compounded its problems. The Great Depression turned most countries inward, unleashing protectionist impulses and drowning calls for open trade. The rise of fascist regimes in Europe and elsewhere added a tragic political liability to the economic ones. The world swirled in a downward spiral from which the League could not hope to escape. The result was a retreat, spatially as well as normatively and ideationally, from intergovernmental organizations as a core of global governance toward an interwar system of world-order management in which autarky was a key organizing principle. It is fair to say that both the League and its sister institutions were ahead of the curve in terms of institutionalized global governance but behind in Keynesian terms, which fostered subsequent learning about economic measures that took place by the end of World War II.[17]

Second Try at World Organization

As we stated already, the League of Nations failed; but the idea that an international organization could be created to help secure peace was not lost with its demise. During World War II, the Allies decided to try again, this time correcting the perceived flaws of the first experiment with a universal membership world organization. The dominance of the major powers would be enshrined in a Security Council; and the organization's remit would be much more extensive, ranging far beyond peace and security. The result was the creation, in 1945, of the United Nations and shortly thereafter of the more technical bodies of the UN system.

The difficulties of separating continuity from change is obvious from the final session of the League's Assembly in 1946, at which one of its founders and ardent defenders, Lord Robert Cecil, uttered his memorable sound bite: "The League of Nations is dead; long live the United Nations." It is striking how many of the supposedly discredited ideas associated with the defunct League reappeared.[18] Leland Goodrich, a member of the US delegation, explained: "Quite clearly there was a hesitancy in many quarters to call attention to the continuity of the old League and the new United Nations for fear of arousing latent hostilities or creating doubts which might seriously jeopardize the birth and early success of the new organization."[19]

Unlike the post-war architects of the League of Nations, the Allies after World War II had building blocks and decided upon the United Nations long before the end of armed conflict. Indeed, they decided very early – shortly after the United States had entered the war in December 1941 – to establish a major international organization, with more breadth than the League, by the war's end. The intention was to enable the Allies to extend their cooperative activities beyond wartime in order to foster peace as well as prosperity and stability.

Yet, not all of the wartime leaders initially favored the creation of a global organization to replace the League of Nations. The British prime minister, Winston Churchill, initially envisaged a system of regional councils, and the US president, Franklin D. Roosevelt, was at first inclined to agree. However, fearing a repeat of the 1930s, the US secretary of state Cordell Hull thought otherwise and persuaded Roosevelt that a regional system might result in the creation of great power spheres of influence that would lead to discrimination against US trade. Churchill eventually followed suit.

While the discussions and planning during World War II took in much, but not all, of the world, they were far from planetary in reach, representation, or involvement. In August 1941, Churchill and Roosevelt agreed in principle on the name of "the United Nations" and signed the Atlantic Charter. On 1 January 1942, twenty-six governments signed the Declaration by United Nations in Washington, DC, calling for mutual support among the Allies and a more permanent system to maintain international peace and security. At the same time they committed to repel the forces of Germany, Italy, and Japan. In November 1943, just a few weeks before his first meeting with the Soviet premier, Josef Stalin, in Tehran, Roosevelt declared at a White House conference that "We mean business in this war in a political and humanitarian sense just as surely as we mean business in a military sense."[20] The 1943 Moscow Four-Nation Declaration consolidated this commitment to the continuation of cooperation into the post-war period. And the development of the post-war United Nations then evolved through conferences in Dumbarton Oaks (August–October 1944), Yalta (February 1945), and San Francisco (April–June 1945).

Between 1943 and 1947 the Allied commitment to defeating fascism was on display not only through military campaigns in Europe, Asia, and North Africa, but also through the first operational humanitarian manifestation of that commitment in the United Nations Relief and Rehabilitation Administration (UNRRA). Intense planning was also under way in other fields, ranging from education to trade and from agriculture to aviation. The scale of commitment and planning was impressive, and the consequence was to extend from the outset the reach of this aspect of a new system of global governance.[21]

Global Governance through Regionalization

Yet, almost as World War II concluded the Cold War broke out. One immediate consequence was to paralyze the security functions of the UN. With deadlock in the Security Council, the Eastern and Western blocs sought to consolidate their respective spheres of influence. The result was a spatial bifurcation in the emerging post-war order. Part of the process involved the creation of regional economic and security organizations.

The Marshall Plan's aid to Western Europe and Scandinavia in 1947 began this process and drew lines of demarcation between the superpower blocs. The funds from the Marshall Plan were disbursed to those countries that were interested in reconstructing their economies along Western lines. The allocation of aid was to be overseen by the Organisation for European Economic Co-operation, later to become the Organisation for Economic Co-operation and Development (OECD). The Soviet Union sponsored the Warsaw Pact and the Council for Mutual Economic Assistance (also known as COMECON), and the United States sponsored the North Atlantic Treaty Organization (NATO) and fostered cooperation in the European Economic Community (EEC).

The move to create regional organizations was not confined to the Eastern and Western blocs, however. During the 1950s, 1960s, and 1970s many of the world's colonies gained independence and established international organizations of their own. Most significant among these organizations were the NAM, the G77, and the United Nations Conference on Trade and Development (UNCTAD). The consolidation of distinct spheres of influence was enhanced by those international economic organizations that had been created to reconstruct the global economy – the IMF, the World Bank, and the GATT. These institutions, although not formally closed to Eastern bloc membership, serviced primarily Western bloc members as well as newly independent countries.

The consequence of this process of institution-building in three regional blocs was to extend post-war global governance worldwide. Common to all areas was the deployment of international institutions as nodes of control and regulation. Superpower competition provided the material underpinnings. Ideology – capitalist, communist, non-aligned – lent the system its organizing principles.

The end of the Cold War did not put an end to this system or the role played by regional organizations. A second round led to regional political and economic institutions extending further the spatial reach of this component of global governance, with the consequences that the overall system became further embedded. Examples from this second bout included the African Union (AU), earlier founded as the Organization of African Unity (OAU), the Association of Southeast Asian Nations (ASEAN), the Organization of American States (OAS), the South Asian Association for Regional Cooperation (SAARC), and the Arab League. Elsewhere, the end of the Cold War eased the paralysis that had afflicted the UN. The Warsaw Pact and COMECON disbanded. The former Soviet bloc and newly independent countries joined Western regional and international organizations. And pre-existing regional organizations deepened the extent of their cooperation, with Europe notably expanding and deepening its integration project with the creation and subsequent extension of the European Union.

The story of what happened to global governance after the end of the Cold War is one that we have addressed elsewhere in this book. What is important for our purposes here is that sketching the intergovernmental foundations of our current order has illustrated how this aspect of contemporary global governance has evolved spatially and highlighted its evolving complexity and density. Moreover, it is worth emphasizing that all of these organizations were evolved forms of political organization burgeoning in the industrial (and industrializing) world before the outbreak of World War I. They were developments of the nineteenth-century order that carried forward familiar ways of arranging relations among the Western powers, mechanisms of controlling the lands and the people subjected to European domination, and the remnants of inter-imperial balance of power. At the same time, they challenged that order, in terms of its general arrangement as well as in the principles and practices for the future governance of world order. We might also point out that the inter-imperial order was itself the consequence of elements of continuity and change of earlier systems of world order. Only an excavation of these evolutionary processes will enable us to get a proper handle on global governance across time and space.

Conclusion: Continuing the Journey

Over the course of the past century and a half, state-based international institutions have consistently shaped - sometimes profoundly so - the global governance that we currently have. Yet, the paradox is that most of those that we know best are not the ones that have a daily impact on our lives. Behind the headline organizations - the UN, IMF, World Bank, and WTO - work a myriad of less visible bodies. These organizations are often engaged in technical, behind-the-scenes activities - such as setting standards, harmonizing intellectual property regimes, stopping the spread of disease - and they have an important effect on the way that the world is governed.

Without these institutions and the activities in which they engage, we might not have the railway gauges that enable trains to cross national borders, the capacity to transmit money worldwide, or nuts and bolts in familiar and useful sizes. We may also have had more conflict, less trade, lower prosperity, and, almost certainly, lower global connectivity. We would, in brief, be in a more isolated place.

With the work of these organizations has come greater closeness in a physical sense as well as in perceptions. This closeness has brought with it an extension of the reach and capacity of intergovernmental frameworks – as well as of other global governance actors and machineries. The extension of the Internet, for example, has facilitated the reach of regulatory regimes that shape virtual activity and behavior, such as that convened by ICANN. In turn, they have helped facilitate further worldwide penetration of digital media. In earlier times, we might think of the telegram, telephone, and postal service and their attendant regulatory bodies – the International Telecommunication Union (ITU) and the International Postal Union (IPU) – in a similar regard. Both the earlier and later generations of technical organizations have adapted and form part of global governance's contemporary mosaic.

Of course, not all intergovernmental institutions arose simply to advance communications and technologies. Some were constructed in ways that spoke more to the interests of the dominant powers than to those of the collective; and many still function in ways that reflect those initial purposes. Moreover, many have failed – sometimes miserably so – in stopping the kinds of catastrophes that they were designed to arrest; and they have been implicated in the spread of ideas and ideologies that have created inequalities, embedded discrimination, and reified malpractice. Often their lack of effectiveness is the consequence of the actions and activities of the member states that dominate them. Others have problematic institutional structures that require reform, and most have remits and mandates that have "crept" beyond that which was originally imagined – for good or bad.

What is clear, however, is that, as a center-piece of the contemporary system of global governance, international organization is firmly established and – in the absence of a dramatic shift in global relations of power[22] – international institutions are likely to become more rather than less visible features of world politics. However, they are also clearly evolutions of institutional forms established at key moments in time that did not have the reach that they have today or will need to have tomorrow. They often built upon or departed from earlier efforts to lend coherence to a particular issue, but they were involved in the management of world order nonetheless.

Our aim in this chapter has been to show how global governance, correctly imagined, is applicable not just to the last three decades but also to world orders whose coverage was less than worldwide. If planetary really isn't the point, as this chapter's title suggests, our unfinished journey could and should be extended back to orders other than our own. Looking back to understand and reframe the temporal and spatial dimensions of global governance is not our only motivation, however. Given what we know of the past, we can reasonably ask: What might future systems of global governance resemble? Will they result from unnecessary and unspeakable tragedies, as the United Nations and many of its intergovernmental brethren did from the ashes of World War II? Is, as Frantz Fanon claimed, the replacement of one order necessarily a violent phenomenon?[23] Could more robust institutions result from learning lessons about how best to address needs that clearly do not respect borders but that evolve from evolutions of, rather than departures from, pre-existing systems?

These questions are unnerving because cataclysms are the customary currency for global institutional reforms. Nonetheless, a human capacity exists for learning and adapting; it is unnecessary to await suffering on a scale that could well dwarf that of World War II. We should thus not act as if today's international political order were immutable and pre-ordained and the provision of global public goods a fool's errand.

We return to these and other questions in the conclusion to the book. Before we do, however, we need to explore the importance of adding one further piece to the global governance puzzle: the view from below.

4

Global Governance in
the Everyday

In his 1946 plenary address to the Association of American
Geographers, John K. Wright observed that

> whether or not a particular area may be called "unknown" depends
> both on whose knowledge and on what kind of knowledge is taken
> into account . . . [O]n the early European maps, the words *terra
> incognita* signified a land unknown to the map maker . . . but if such
> "unknown territories" were beyond the ken of the geographers and
> cartographers of Western civilization, they were known to their
> inhabitants . . . China lay deep in the heart of *terra incognita* to
> the Romans, but the Roman Empire was equally lost in "unknown
> land" to the Chinese.

Wright was keen to point out that *terrae incognitae* were not confined to understandings of geographical space alone. "[T]here are
personal, community, and national *terrae incognitae*: there are
the *terrae incognitae* to different cultural traditions and civiliza-

tions; and there are also the *terrae incognitae* to contemporary geographical science."[1]

While Wright's observations about the subjective, contextual, and situational nature of knowledge are hardly revelatory for contemporary social science, they offer a useful way of thinking about the third of three missing elements that are essential to achieving a more satisfactory understanding of global governance. Throughout the book, we have noted that much of our current understanding of global governance is shaped by what we know, and a great deal of our reluctance to wrest it from the common associations that have hampered its analytical utility result from a lack of knowledge and appreciation of other views. We see this shortcoming in the discussions of time and space in the two preceding chapters. Yet, we have so far omitted questions about how global governance is perceived and received by others, particularly by those not involved in its creation or function but whose lives are shaped, sometimes intimately so, by its operation.

In this chapter, we discuss the importance of understanding global governance from the view not just of those who govern but also of those who are on its receiving end. In so doing, we seek to confine one more *terra incognita* in studies of global governance to the annals of intellectual history. Our claim is that time and space are not the only missing elements required of a more nourishing conception of global governance. Also neglected are understandings of global governance in the everyday – that is, accounts of the daily experiences of those whose lives are affected by the myriad ways that world order is fashioned and governed.

We contend that global governance is far starker in the everyday than is usually acknowledged. We should consider for a moment the effect that international borders – a key means by which order is lent to the contemporary world and a technology of governance and control noted earlier – have on everyday life. International borders shape relations between communities, and not just those who find themselves bifurcated by boundaries – such as Kurds in Iraq, Iran, Syria, and Turkey or families seeking refuge in the United States from violence in Central America. Boundaries also have an impact on those whose commerce and communications require transboundary passages – such as Syrian shepherds in the Israeli-occupied Golan Heights. Likewise, alterations to international borders and rules governing movements across them (of goods, services, and people) have a profound effect. The changes wrought by the UK's departure from the EU – in passing from the Republic of Ireland to Northern Ireland and in travelling to and from the UK to continental Europe – are one example among many.

Our aim, thus, is to reverse the usual top-down analytical lens and consider how global governance generally, as well as discrete elements within particular systems, are seen from the bottom up – that is, from the perspective of the "globally governed." When viewed from this direction, we discover a perspective that is all too often absent; we are then able to feed back into analyses in ways that have so far been eschewed, or at least overlooked. This, in turn, enables us to lend further precision to thinking about what is required to bring about effective and lasting change.

In pursuit of our aims, the chapter unfolds as follows. The next section explores why this approach has so far been *terra incognita* in the literature on global governance. We then parse three examples that illustrate the way that global governance shapes everyday life, thereby bringing this little-known terrain front and center to thinking in the field. In so doing, we note the limited capacity of most individuals and peoples to have a say in the management systems that exist beyond their locales and countries but have a profound effect on their existence. The final section offers some concluding comments as a prelude to the final chapter.

Looking from the Bottom Up is Harder than from the Top Down

Why do we not know more than we do about global governance in the everyday? We know a great deal about the power of financial markets because the effects of catastrophic financial collapse have animated the work of scholars after every major economic collapse – of which the 2008 global financial crisis is only the most recent. Yet, we do not know nearly enough about how precisely global financial decision-making affects daily life. We are far from an understanding of the relationship between what transpires in Zurich and London and household income quakes on the ground for farmers in the Andes or the Great Plains, or the connections between the speculative actions of traders in global commodity markets and the effects on local spot markets and farming livelihoods. The best that we can probably say is that financial and economic crises render the everyday lives of ordinary people more precarious, with those living in the Global South likely to be the most affected.

These oversights are of course not the preserve of our understandings of global financial systems alone. We are equally remiss in failing to comprehend the everyday effects of international assistance programs or crisis responses, or of health restrictions put in place in response to an outbreak of infectious disease and the impact their subsequent removal has on the capacity of communities to re-establish commerce. Suffice to say that all too often we have failed to explore how the globally governed have encountered - that is, received and experienced, for good and for ill - global governance. Instead, we have concentrated on the actions and activities of those who govern the globe. The result is that enduring images of global governance are of international bureaucracies in New York and Geneva, world conferences in major capital cities on issues of planetary significance, corporate boardrooms in marquee buildings, and geopolitical wrangles over appointees to key positions in international organizations, corporations, and governments. They are not of refugees in Breidjing, grain traders in Khanna, or sex workers in Tijuana. Yet, the lives of these people are severely affected by multiple aspects of contemporary global governance, as are those of a multitude of others.

Why are the globally governed so invisible in our analyses?[2] Conceptually - as we pointed out earlier - it is certainly the case that the close association between the term "global governance" and what international organizations do has overly determined the extent to which the field has proceeded along an evolutionary path wherein the words "global" and "governance" have become descriptors for the collective activities, accomplishments, and failures of intergovernmental institutions. Our political and analytical attention has followed. But it may also be that our tendency to read global governance - its history, content, and drivers of change - from the vantage points of Washington, London, Brussels, or Geneva, and not the community centers of Ruhororo, Burundi, Ürümqi, China, or Dili, Timor-Leste, has compounded matters and concentrated minds on the art of governance rather than its consequences, on the governors rather than the governed. This may reflect the origins and locations of those who study global governance – namely from countries at the center of global decision-making whose analytical radars are insufficiently tuned to looking at the multiple variables in the governance equation, and whose physical distance is far removed from many of the consumers of global governance.

Equally, it is also the case that conducting interviews in world-class cities and exploring archives in well-situated research libraries is far easier than hiring Land Rovers and interpreters, getting inoculations and malaria tablets, and running risks in unknown neighborhoods. Indeed, studying those on the receiving end of global governance can require the kind of fieldwork and investigation into primary sources for which few international relations scholars or prospective students are equipped.[3] We have much to learn from anthropologists whose careers are devoted to comprehending the everyday, often in communities far removed in distance and culture from classrooms, library stacks, and data sets.

That said, global governance scholarship is not, in fact, all that different from research in other disciplines. Most social scientists tend to focus on the most visible institutions and individuals at the center of global problem-solving and policy-making. They customarily stop short of understanding how power and influence flow outwards to recipients. Most of us, particularly in the digital era, have access to primary documents and even interviews at the press of a button. Few have the time, the resources, the language skills, the inclination, or the courage to risk their lives in war zones, go to makeshift customs houses abutting contested international borders, build social networks in isolated communities, or wander into volatile borderlands. The result is that we have restricted global governance largely to questions of institutional design and construction and to policy development and delivery. Absent is how global governance is encountered by those on the ground. To be comprehensive, or even make sense, global governance must address these empirical and experiential shortcomings.

There are other reasons why we should correct this gaping oversight in our analytical industry. As we have already indicated, much of the practice of governing globally originates in the Global North. This is – to paraphrase Deborah Avant, Martha Finnemore, and Susan Sell – where most of the "global governors" reside, work, and play.[4] In contrast, many of the recipients of contemporary global governance are in the Global South, and its most acute effects are often experienced by the most vulnerable citizens (women, children, the elderly, and indigenous peoples). This reality does not mean that the effects of, and strong perceptions about, global governance are absent in the Global North. Indeed, disgruntled voters demonstrated this amply in 2016 in the referendum result on the UK's membership of the EU and the election of Donald Trump as the 45th president of the United States.

These and other examples notwithstanding, it remains the case that many of the world's most precarious communities have a more intimate daily relationship with global governance than do citizens of states where the global governors reside. The intimacy comes via, among many others, the World Bank, the IMF, the Office of the UN High Commissioner for Refugees (UNHCR), the WHO, Oxfam, the International Federation of Red Cross and Red Crescent Societies, and Médecins Sans Frontières (MSF). It comes not only from these recognizable players in contemporary global governance but also from connections with less commonly associated and often such less visible elements as transnational criminal networks, faith groups, and financial markets.

Moreover, those populations on the receiving end of global governance seldom have access to, or a say in, the decision-making whose consequences affect their daily existence. This startling imbalance – along with the vantage points from which we customarily view global governance – is more pronounced when we concentrate on the design and consequences of such institutions. Indeed, because we have studied the successes, failures, and impacts of global governance so narrowly, we may have been complicit in perpetuating outmoded and ineffectual systems. We may also have used perspectives that ignore recipients and their plights as well as restrict and constrain their agency.

Thus, our aim is to attenuate conceptual shortcomings by removing our blinders and bringing the globally governed to the fore. This appeal is akin to the previous clarion calls sounded for international relations, international political economy, and peace studies for the "everyday" to be front and center.[5] It is the final one of our pleas for greater sensitivity, which is to be added to issues of complexity, time, space, continuity, and change that we have so far outlined.

Everyday Global Governance: Three Illustrations

We are not the first to use the term "everyday" global governance. As far as we can tell, Anne-Marie Slaughter holds that honor. However, she used it to describe a different phenomenon from that which we have in mind.[6] Her concern was the silent but extensive growth of transnational networks, especially among lawyers, and their impact. With the benefit of hindsight, we might suggest that she was observing a "quiet," "under the radar," or "creeping" form of global governance,[7] one that is hard to quantify and that evolves independently or quasi-independently of formal governmental and intergovernmental processes. Slaughter was referring not to the actual experience of being governed but, rather, to the informal networks that were contributing to the governing. Her insights are useful but do not help understand how global governance is actually experienced. While her work was at the forefront of early twenty-first-century thinking, it did not look through the other end of the looking glass. The receipt of global governance, the lived experiences, and the actions and relationships are essential to our understanding of the everyday.

To appreciate everyday global governance requires care in mapping existing governance in a given context. It also necessitates that our other highlighted elements – complexity, time, space, continuity, and change – are taken adequately into account. Thus, such a process should capture the scale and extent of global governance's receipt, identify individual components, and plot the individual and combined effects among the various components. The analytical process should be attentive to the complexity of global governance and not just to the role of international organizations and institutions; it should account for the direct and indirect, the formal and informal aspects. Moreover, it requires understanding the forms of behavior to which specific governance contexts give rise – here we require an appreciation of the effects on recipients' behavior resulting from the individual and collective aspects of global governance. The analysis also necessitates grasping over time the patterns of change and continuity in local contexts and behaviors. Likewise, some understanding is required of the capacity of those governed to influence the shape, weight, and impact of the governance of which they are on the receiving end.

We illustrate what everyday global governance means with three examples: refugees in Breidjing, Chad; grain traders in Khanna, India; and sex workers in Tijuana, Mexico. We are keen to stress, however, that these examples are far from unusual. Indeed, it is hard to imagine examples of people for whom global governance does *not* have profound daily effects. We could, for instance, have selected indigenous communities in the Amazon whose access to and use of naturally occurring plants collide with and are affected by the drug patent applications of transnational pharmaceutical corporations. We could also have examined Bangladeshi oil workers in Yemen whose daily lives reflect decisions by international cartels and geostrategic regional and global alliances, as well as by IMF structural adjustment programs. We could have focused on working women and men in New Jersey whose capacity to repay and borrow and to keep their own homes as well as to maintain and aspire to improved lives was – and continues to be – shaped dramatically by the fallout from and new rules introduced in response to the 2007–8 global financial crisis.

Our efforts are thus illustrative rather than exhaustive. The processes of global governance affect everyone, and so our examples can only hint at its receipt and magnitude in the everyday. Nonetheless, our illustrations provide compelling instances of the variety of ways that some of the world's most precarious communities receive and experience global governance. Moreover, while the challenges of establishing a future research agenda that takes proper account of everyday global governance are substantial –

and the ethical issues exceedingly complex – we nonetheless want to push our colleagues and ourselves in this direction.

Breidjing

Understanding global governance in the everyday in Breidjing requires trying to understand the regional and domestic sources of the long-standing civil war in the South of Sudan, in addition to the more recent ones from the slow-motion genocide in Darfur, which produced many of Breidjing's refugees. Understanding the dynamics of this largest refugee camp in neighboring Chad also entails tracing the outside peacekeepers from the AU and the UN as well as the actions and inactions by such intergovernmental decision-making bodies as the AU Peace and Security Council, the UN Security Council, and the International Criminal Court (ICC). Of pertinence would also be arms sales and transfers mixed with the political economy of an environmentally threatened Sudan and its interactions with world markets, especially in oil and cotton.

These top-down elements are familiar, albeit overwhelmingly difficult to weave together in a complete and coherent portrait. Appreciating their impact, nonetheless, also necessitates an investigation of the life experiences molded by residing in a UNHCR-run camp. In addition, we need to map how the policies, programs, and activities of that UN body and its governing council and major donors relate to the actions of a host of such other intergovernmental bodies as the World Food Programme (WFP), UNICEF, the International Organization for Migration (IOM), and the UN Office for the Coordination of Humanitarian Affairs (OCHA). Clear distinctions should characterize the variety of effects of such agencies on everyday life, recognizing that some have a power-ful impact on everyday experiences while others are indirect but nonetheless significant. For instance, as the coordinating agency for the camp's organization and administration, UNHCR oversees many of the details of daily existence. OCHA's capacity to bring together coalitions of aid agencies and donors also affects not only the speed, type, and magnitude of responses but also the plans for medium- to longer-term settlement, resettlement, education, training, and, ultimately, a hoped-for return to development.

Beyond this intergovernmental core, lives in Breidjing are shaped by the actions of a host of general-purpose and dedicated humanitarian NGOs – which in Chad include CARE International, Oxfam, the ICRC and the Red Cross of Chad, the Hebrew Immigrant Aid Society, the Gesellschaft für Internationale Zusammenarbeit Committee, and the Lutheran World Federation, among many others, large and small. And, of course, the lives of refugees – who are overwhelmingly women, children and the elderly – also are shaped by their relationships with insurgent and paramilitary forces.

Within camps, the organization of daily life begins with crisis responses: combating the spread of diseases such as cholera, malaria, and hepatitis E; establishing access to food and water, sanitation, and medical supplies; and providing shelter and temporary accommodation. As a camp becomes more estab-lished, a new phase begins, and life experiences steadily diverge. Administrative structures delineate "official" refugees from their "unofficial" and unregistered counterparts. While the lives of the former are hardly easy, registration at least brings certain rights to rations of food, water, and firewood as well as access to basic services and identity papers. For the unregistered, life is even more precarious than for their registered compatriots. Those not formally recognized by camp officials are obliged more frequently to search for firewood outside of the formal boundaries of the site, which places women and girls particularly at risk from kidnapping, sexual harassment, assault, and rape.

The consequences of being a recipient of, or excluded from, a specific global governance program are manifest. For instance, children born to registered refugees receive birth certificates as markers of existence, citizenship, rights, and entitlements. They likely reside in the better tents, are the first in the queue for medical treatment, and eventually gain access to limited education. In contrast, those born to unregistered refugees live in makeshift structures rather than UNHCR-provided tents, fare less well, are potentially stateless, and are without access to what little life-improving opportunities may be available to their registered counterparts. Their lives are also likely to be exploited by those nefarious actors who take advantage of failures and omissions in the provision of public goods by international organizations of all kinds. Those geographically and administratively farther away from the safety net provided by humanitarian agencies are more likely to fall prey to insurgents and paramilitary groups, health crises, and shortages in essential goods. Moreover, the longer that it takes to broker a truce, let alone a lasting solution to an armed conflict – often under the auspices of IGOs – the more likely that the already vulnerable will confront even more pernicious aspects of global governance. For instance, one indication is the limited attention spans and donor fatigue, as many "emergencies" have become preceded by the oxymoron adjective "permanent" (so called after five years).

Other external factors also have a bearing on the everyday global governance of Breidjing's denizens. Financial crises affect donor willingness to fund relief missions; they partially explain the growing shortfalls in funding, which in turn – as happened following the 2008 financial crisis – reduce the size of food rations and medicine.[8] The willingness and success of international actors to address the sources of refugee flight are also pertinent. Longer-term solutions for an enduring peace in Sudan remain a distant hope to enable refugees and internally displaced persons to return home or be resettled permanently in a third country. Likewise, the more entrenched a war, especially when coupled with violence elsewhere in the region, the more likely that donor attention will be diverted toward newer, "louder," and more visible emergencies. Other factors still should enter our thick description: the influence of traffickers and gangs; counterfeit registration systems; brain drains from local actors to outside humanitarian agencies; soaring local rents; and parallel economies, in both global and local marketplaces.[9] When viewed from the perspective of desperate refugees whose lives depend on the direct and daily efforts by a host of actors, the tentacles of global governance seem powerful and all encompassing.

Khanna

For a grain trader in Khanna, Asia's largest market, the everyday effects of global governance are different from those of a refugee, but the analytical impact is no less challenging – and certainly no less complex and arduous to decipher. While we commonly recognize that the cost of our own grocery basket reflects global trade rules and such related effects as inflation, we are less likely to think about how they influence the lives of Khanna's traders. Equally, we are less likely to take into account how long-run historical events – including the annexation of Punjab by the British East India Company in the mid-nineteenth century, the struggle for independence, partition, and ongoing regional geopolitics – have shaped livelihoods in that part of India.[10] Yet, to complete our understanding of everyday global governance, we are obliged to situate our investigation within this wider context.

Global governance for grain traders comes via commodity markets that are local, national, regional, and global. The behavior of traders is shaped by the rules governing those markets – by who is allowed to trade, the social networks that facilitate access, where grain is stored, the systems used for quality control, and health regulations. Market performance, financial crises, and a host of factors ranging from exchange rates to fluctuations in credit directly hurt or help their livelihoods. However, their involvement in the various webs of global governance does not end with the local application of international trade rules and an understanding of their place in a complex variety (both sizes and locations) of markets. Although farmers are linked to the Khanna grain market through procurement agencies and private buyers who sell their crops, local producers are also subject to influences other than the market. Many participate in commercial microfinance schemes or those underwritten by the World Bank. They may have been recipients of FAO projects and training programs designed to boost production, or of related efforts to enhance nutrition, livelihoods, rural development, and sustainability. Moreover, they may be part of FAO-assisted national regimes for pest control or climate-change mitigation. In addition, bilateral donors and international NGOs may have mounted similar efforts.

More broadly, the effects of other national programs in which India participates also have a direct impact upon on the lives of

Khanna's grain traders and rural farmers. The effects may ema-
nate from reforms required by IMF country-level agreements; the
implementation and roll-out of the 2030 SDGs; New Delhi's efforts
to gain an exemption for its national food-security legislation from
WTO commitments;[11] or WHO and UNICEF projects targeted at
improving health and education in rural areas. India's involvement in these aspects of multilateralism is implemented alongside
established relations with bilateral donors such as the operational
plan of the UK's Department for International Development
(DfID) and the work that overseas development agencies carry out
in partnership with such NGOs as the US government's partnership with the Society for Research and Initiatives for Sustainable
Technologies and Institutions.

Equally, the lives of Indian farmers and grain traders are
shaped by the delivery of global programs to reverse adverse climate change, including measures necessary to make good on the
December 2015 Paris Agreement (and the successes or failures
thereof). Lives and livelihoods are directly affected by the capacity of international programs to buttress adverse climate-induced
incidents or to invest in measures to prevent catastrophes or limit
their impact. In addition, lives and livelihoods are also influenced
by the longer-term effects of scientific advancements and (the
politics of) the use of new fertilizers, pest control, irrigation systems, agricultural mechanization, and measures to counter crop
diseases. They reflect programs that seek to promote other goals
that rupture and change social relations on the ground: education and gender empowerment, good governance, democratic
representation, and the end to such internationally condemned
practices as female infanticide and honor killings.[12] And the lives of
Indian farmers and grain traders are also shaped by international

assistance and commecial ventures that facilitate mobile bank-ing and the flow of remittances; WFP, UNDP, and IMF national programs; the activities of myriad NGOs; and the implementation of MDG and SDG projects and programs, among many others.

As with Breidjing's refugees, access to and exclusion from vari-ous global programs for assistance, credit, and investment shapes the lives of Khanna's farmers and grain traders. Those excluded have little or no access. Their prospects diverge distinctly from those with access to local markets, who are recipients of FAO-supported national programs to promote diversification away from grain farming to aquaculture (largely carp fish farming); have direct or indirect aid from bilateral assistance programs (such as the USAID–Bill and Melinda Gates Foundation's Cereal System Initiative or DfID's infrastructure, inclusive growth, edu-cation, innovation, housing, and skills development programs); or benefit from the efforts of myriad international or civil soci-ety organizations. Again, those of us reading or writing about global governance can debate the wide range of theoretical and normative implications, but Khanna's farmers and grain traders experience global governance in their everyday existence.

Tijuana

Exploring the lives of sex workers in Tijuana, Mexico, illustrates further the differing experiences of the globally governed. It also reflects the looming effects of possible changes in contemporary global governance resulting from the administration of US presi-dent Donald Trump – including attempts to build a wall on the southern US border, a stated intention to renegotiate NAFTA, a changing immigration regime, the impact of currency fluctuations, the imposition of trade-diverting tariffs on Mexican goods, and the July 2018 election of the populist president Andrés Manuel López Obrador.[13] Although sex workers on the US–Mexico border are perhaps less visible than Breidjing's refugees and Khanna's farmers and grain traders, many dimensions of global governance are comparable. Researching their plight also brings challenges not encountered in other illustrations. Blended with the obvious precariousness encountered by sex workers, they provide a compelling optic through which to comprehend different and frequently painful aspects of everyday global governance.

Here the complexity of global governance goes far beyond the roles of IGOs and NGOs. In particular, the character of Mexico's economic, political, and cultural relations with the United States and its immigration policies weigh mightily. How NAFTA is revisited, the peso's exchange rate, the effect of tariffs, additional physical boundaries, and more muscular anti-immigration regimes are factors that have not been as poignant variables in the two earlier cases. Nonetheless, the direct and indirect, formal and informal aspects of global governance must be carefully identified and their relationships judiciously understood. The effects should be disaggregated so that discrete aspects are understood as well as their sum, the patterns of change and continuity in both the local context and behavior over time are appreciated, and the capacity of sex workers to influence the shape and impact of the global governance they receive understood.

So how might a researcher proceed? To be effective, an investigation into everyday global governance in the sex industry in Tijuana would situate it as a significantly gendered, barely legal, and unevenly regulated economic activity. In large measure, demand is stimulated by the city's proximity to an international border and where supply reflects – among many things – forced participation, trafficking, and slavery. In turn, the nature of this market requires understanding the development of sex work in Mexico and the United States as well as in border regions between the two countries and sensitive legal, political, and economic factors. It also requires understanding the particular political economy of a local area, including the trafficking and regulation of drugs. It necessitates grappling with the wider political economy in which they are enmeshed. Furthermore, it necessitates a sensitivity to the broader geopolitics of US–Mexican relations on the demand for sex work, the supply of ancillary services (such as sexual health care), and prevailing ideas about the value, moral purpose, and organization of the sex industry.

The various actors and institutions shaping the lives of sex workers in Tijuana and their respective formal or informal roles, as direct or indirect agents, are harder to map and hardly the typical bill of fare for global governance scholars.[14] Thus, documenting and comprehending suppliers and clients – their history, rationale, culture, and evolution – as well as the precariousness of sex workers' lives requires examining the means (forcible or otherwise) by which workers are brought to Tijuana and engaged (again, forcibly or otherwise) in the sex industry. It necessitates understanding the WHO's sexual health programs, the impact of university research to observe the effect of microfinance initiatives, the impact of the educational efforts by the UN Office on Drugs and Crime, the economic fortunes of companies in the region whose workers are clients, and the role and effects of religious groups in promoting or resisting particular sexual health efforts. It also requires understanding the flow of immigrants fleeing from violence in the Northern Triangle of Central America through Mexico, who seek refuge in the United States but who may be stranded at the border.

Care and attention is required in identifying individuals and groups for case studies. Any conclusions or propositions should be tempered by a consideration of specific time periods that could substantially alter aspects of global governance – such as the passage of new trans-border legislation, health-care programs, or clampdowns on transnational trafficking and criminal activity. The spatial aspects of sex work – not just the features and changes in the industry's local geography but also the transnational and international aspects of trafficking, remittances, financial flows, credit schemes, and HIV/AIDS programs – are especially problematic. The Tijuana sex workers provide a compelling illustration of our call for more field-based research in IR scholarship; they also throw up some of the thorniest issues, particularly with regard to the effective protection of sex workers and researchers alike.

We also see marked differences between those who benefit from particular aspects of global governance and those who do not. Those with access to sexual health and drug rehabilitation activities provided by IGOs and NGOs are likely to fare better than those excluded or prevented from participating. Those caught up in the more nefarious aspects of global governance – for instance, sex workers trafficked by gangs that may or may not also be involved in illicit money-laundering, drugs, and guns – have life experiences dramatically different still. Piecing such experiences together and situating them alongside those of others among the globally governed helps us to understand the effects of how the world is ordered. This better understanding should then enable us to work out more appropriate forms of governance that result in improved global, regional, national, and local public policies.

In this way, such inquiries should also help recapture some of the lost normative project of early contributions to the field.[15]

Conclusion: The Bottom-Up Speaks

Our purpose has been to set out the necessity and utility of looking up at global governance from the point of view of those who are globally governed – literally peering through the other end of Alice's looking glass. This perspective is distinct from the top-down approaches that have largely predominated in the field. We truly need to know much more about how the world is governed; how we have ended up with our current governance arrangements; what kind of global governance we ought to have; and how we could get from here to there.

As social scientists, we are supposed to ask, "So what?" The answer at the end of this chapter is obvious: adding the dimension of the globally governed is essential to sketch better the pluses and minuses of any macro-policies of global governance and also to identify appropriate means to improve individual lives. We have emphasized three examples from the Global South, but we have indicated the imperative to understand those experiencing the downsides of globalization and global governance at all levels – in industrialized as well as developing countries.

In order to overcome claims that global governance is too nebulous, an ambitious future research agenda requires looking toward overcoming the absence of feedback loops and the presence of path dependency, and more especially reducing the accountability gaps between the governors and the governed. Indeed, perhaps the most crucial lacuna that emerges from these illustrations is the total absence of voices of the globally governed in the origins, administration, and follow-up for the programs and actions that have a dramatic influence on lives in Breidjing, Khanna, and Tijuana. While some experiences of what happens on the ground do filter upwards to policy- and decision-makers in capital cities and headquarters, local perspectives are at best diluted or at worst missing in the perspectives of the global governors whose focus is invariably on the macro. Yet, the absence of adequate representation ensures curtailing or excluding the recipients from having a say in the systems of governance that shape their lives. It is to thinking about how we bring all of this together and make global governance better analytically and practically that we now turn.

5

Better and Better
Global Governance

The preceding chapters continually noted the excessively close association between the term "global governance" and what international organizations do – an approach that has overly determined the extent to which our field has proceeded in a path-dependent fashion. This association has joined at the hip "global" and "governance" to connote collective problem-solving by IGOs and NGOs in the post-Cold War era. While international organizations are perhaps the most visible and certainly a crucial part of contemporary world order, they are not the whole story. As a result, the analysis of global governance has been too anchored in a specific historic moment from which it needs wresting. We proposed moving beyond ahistoricism and planetary space to indicate that, with the right questions, global governance should provide insights into the ways that world orders are governed and ordered in all periods irrespective of the extent of their geographical coverage. Finally, in exploring how global governance is encountered by individuals in Breidjing, Khanna, and Tijuana, we have argued that we should struggle to comprehend all aspects and perspectives on global governance; we cannot ignore the individuals who "consume" and are subjected to the products of today's world order.

Thus, we have sought to move the concept of global governance beyond a simple association with international organization and law, multilateralism, and what states have done in concert over the last three decades. We are seeking to advance a framework that looks at the way that world orders are organized and governed, the overall context in which interactions take place, and the manner in which humanity conducts its affairs. Simultaneously, we have proposed that we need to pay attention to a host of other formal and informal actors, principles, norms, networks, and mechanisms, while taking seriously the requirements of time, space, and place (what we call the "everyday") in our effort to grapple with global governance and to advance understandings of its complexity as well as its management.

So far, so good. However, we need now to tease out the proposition that global governance actors are not merely involved in the creation and preservation of the status quo but that they are also agents of change. They are thus – albeit in different degrees, because Dow Chemical is not the ICRC, Fox News is not Oxfam – responsible for victors and victims, and they are both able to maintain the status quo and effect a measure of change. This final chapter aims to move our unfinished journey further along a path toward what we believe is a better and crisper intellectual grasp of global governance. In so doing, we also seek a better and more justifiable normative grasp of our elusive subject matter.

Rethinking: The Intellectual Task

As we hope to have made clear, the contemporary study of global governance sprouted and took root among academics and policy wonks in the 1990s, which coincided with the demise of the Cold War. This new-found attention reflected growing global interdependence and rapid technological advances as well as the sheer expansion in numbers and importance of civil society organizations, for-profit corporations, and a host of other – often considerably less salubrious – actors. Our starting point was that the term has come to refer to collective efforts to identify, understand, and address the worldwide problems and processes whose mastery goes beyond the capacities of individual states. It reflected a capacity of the international system to provide some public goods and order – or something like government services – but without any overarching world authority; it encompassed a wide variety of cooperative problem-solving arrangements that were visible but informal and even temporary. The term also captured more formal and formalized legal and institutional structures and practices that sought to manage cooperation among actors ranging from states to IGOs, from NGOs and civil society to businesses.

We pointed to historical change as a fruitful point of departure, especially after realizing that it is not planetary that is the point but, rather, widespread human governance across time. We asked the same kinds of questions that led to understanding global governance as a pluralization of world politics at the end of the last century. We did so to suggest the kinds of systems that made sense in world orders before the current one, and how power and authority were exercised in them. That path of inquiry allowed us to suggest insights about the drivers of change and their impact.

Our claim has been that a deeper investigation of contemporary global governance can suggest accurate outlines for how power is exercised across the globe; how a multiplicity of actors relate to one another generally as well as on specific issues; how to make better sense of complexity; and how to account for alterations in the way that the world is and has been organized and governed over time – both within and between historical periods. Finally, we drew attention to the need to understand how the 7.6 billion-plus denizens of our planet actually experience global governance in their daily lives.

Our explanations of change and continuity across time and space as well as a consideration of everyday global governance point toward the research task ahead: How can we operationalize the concept? How can we have a better empirical grasp of it? An initial step at the end of the beginning of our journey is to under-stand better the dynamics of continuity and change. The answers involve exploring a clutch of crucial dynamics: power, ideas, material capabilities, communications, economics, and security.

This is a daunting task. It requires that others first accept our core proposition: that global governance has existed since separate human communities sought to regularize and govern relations between and among themselves. It also requires that we accept – from the outset – that earlier systems of global governance have not been worldwide in their coverage but nonetheless had a powerful impact on large swathes of the planet's population and geography. Global governance has approached something like worldwide coverage only in the current epoch. The key here is to accept that the large proportion of intercommunity relations have been subject to some form of rule: shaping, constraining, and gov-erning human interactions. We as a community of scholars must accept and seek to comprehend that world orders have existed before our own. We have been even less willing, however, to investigate how those orders have been constructed, negotiated, managed, and ruled – the same questions that we use to understand today's global governance. Equally, we have spent precious little time in trying to understand how those earlier world orders and the forms of governance to which they are subjected have influenced everyday life. Only then will we be able to understand what has and what has not changed in the way that the world is ordered, as well as alterations and continuities in the effects that these systems have on the daily lives of individuals, and how those on the receiving end of global governance could have more of a say in their lives.

To accomplish this task, we first need to ask questions about previous world orders that are designed to understand their character and their internal constitution. We need to understand what the relations of power were upon which they were constructed and the mechanisms that held world orders together. We need to comprehend the ideas – religious, (social) Darwinist, economic, and political – that lent legitimacy and structure to specific formations; how these ideas informed and were influenced by the forms of communication and exchange that existed between settled and unsettled political communities; what forms of commerce and wealth accumulation were present and their ordering effects; how security and stability (or instability) were provided; and what the effects were on those subject to the dominant forms of governance.

These are relatively straightforward – albeit methodologically challenging – questions in our own era. We are able to trace the relations of power that underpin world order in the early twenty-first century. We can identify the main political actors and are able to point to less visible agents and mechanisms in refining our understandings. We are able to comprehend the blend of ideas that legitimize and order our world. We know what forms of communication and intercourse predominate and which shape the macro and the everyday. We have an appreciation of the contemporary world economy, forms of wealth accumulation, and resource distributions. We can trace the primary vectors of security and insecurity.

Moving backwards, we can ask questions about what has changed about our world order along with what preceded it and has influenced contemporary affairs. We can understand, or at least put forward plausible propositions about, the alterations in relations of power, ideas, communications, economy, and security, as well as in their impact on the lives of individuals at all levels. This undertaking is a relatively straightforward task when we explore the global governance of the immediate post-World War II era, but it becomes more difficult for the interregnum of the interwar years, and trickier still for the period that preceded the outbreak of World War I in 1914 and back into the nineteenth century. We have illustrated the way that we might understand how world order was governed; what the dominant relations of power were; what ideas animated and legitimated systems of governance; how communications and intercourse were fashioned; and how the economy and security were manifest within these orders. More work is needed nonetheless.

Evaluating more distant historical epochs, however, is far more problematic. We cannot simply pluck one from the air because of intellectual or other curiosity without first tracing continuities, changes, and mutations as we move back in time with data that are less available than those from today. Thus, understanding the manner in which distant world orders were organized becomes an altogether more uncertain task, especially for social scientists who have limited mastery over and knowledge about the dynamics of earlier historical periods and the world orders that dominated. Moreover, attempting to understand the complexion of actors involved in the governance of world order in, say, the eleventh century and trying to retro-fit them for the modern era – in terms of what has changed, what has not, and why – runs the risk of being ill-informed or even haphazard and arbitrary. These difficulties do not mean that we should check our ambition and refrain from asking tough questions. However, it does suggest that the best way to begin that task is to trace backwards more proximate orders from which today's systems have evolved. This method, for us, seems the most compelling way to understand what we have and how we came by it, and where we are and how we got there. This challenge requires a focus on what has endured and what has changed over the last two centuries as our primary analytical considerations.

This ambition is not, of course, without acute challenges, particularly for amateur historians. Tracing back from the present is likely to be laborious for those keen to understand what systems of global governance existed among and between ancient civilizations. Moreover, it is unlikely to be satisfactory for professional historians or those keen on soon having insights about ancient formations of governance. No matter how problematic or feeble, it is essential to make the attempt if we are to acquire a crisper and more satisfying understanding of global governance, past and present, as well as of how drivers of change and continuity can be manipulated so that future orders do not preserve or re-create the mistakes of the past.

Our endeavor has not been to trace in satisfying detail that empirical journey into world orders past – a task of greater enormity than this book, or the remains of our careers, allows. Rather, it has been immediately to rescue global governance as an analytical device for making sense of the way that the world was and is governed. Wrenching global governance from the contemporary moment and applying it historically and spatially as well as to its recipients is the essence of the conceptual war that we are waging. Yet, we also have an ongoing normative battle.

Rethinking: The Normative Task

The move backwards would have limited salience if it was not also relevant and valuable for understanding tomorrow. We need to keep an eye on how possible future systems of global governance can be adjusted and recrafted to produce fairer outcomes, or at least to attenuate the worst blights that have afflicted world orders past, and how they might be brought about without the catastrophic consequences that have often accompanied world-order transitions. We now turn our attention to the second way that we can "better" global governance.

Our pursuit for a better understanding of the dynamics of global governance has always been much more than an attempt to reconcile the mismatch between the demand for and supply of particular global governance mechanisms in today's world order. We have sought to develop a capacity to prescribe course corrections and formulate strategies for a more stable and just world order. At the turn of the seventeenth century, Francis Bacon argued that "knowledge is power." He also spelled out the basics of induction and inspiration in seeking scientific knowledge. For him, the purpose of science was to improve the common good. The purpose of our social science should be as well.

The reason to seek more knowledge is to be in a position to prescribe how we could make global governance improve the prospects for a more just world order, one in which peace and human rights are realities and not rhetoric, in which sustainable growth and poverty elimination are more than slogans, and in which halting mass atrocities and human rights abuses are actualities and not aspirations. A valid inquiry about global governance should enable us to pursue those objectives by asking more pertinent questions about how the world is organized, how power and authority are exercised, and how adjustments (incremental, wholesale, or otherwise) can be made to make the world a better place.

We need desperately to alter the way that we currently govern the globe – because at this moment planetary is *precisely* the point. That is the scale required for contemporary problem-solving. With refugees and internally displaced persons fleeing in record numbers, the climate changing at alarming rates, WMD circulating, pandemics lurking, and terrorism thriving, we should require no persuading. Transformation is a necessity, not an option; thus, no one should be shy about the use of "ought." It is imperative to frame more specifically "the world we want" (to use the theme song of the SDGs, which the UN General Assembly agreed in September 2015 as setting the development agenda for 2030) and to find paths toward this improved world order.

We simply have to do better in confronting the range of problems that threaten dignified species survival. Our predecessors on planet Earth have often waffled; we cannot. As analysts of global governance, we have failed miserably as agents of change. We have fallen short as purveyors of opinion and of proposals about a better and fairer world. As such, we do not serve well our students and those practitioners who seek our advice; for those of us who take on policy briefs, we no longer push out the envelope far enough to qualify for what passes as acceptable. We too seldom offer a set of tools for understanding how the world works, the grounding on which socially beneficial policy is conceived and implemented. Most importantly, we have not spelled out a comprehensive framework for thinking about substantial changes *of* global governance that are more than the sum of minor adjustments to the operating procedures of specific international organizations and that are able to produce and manage more progressive world orders.

Final Thoughts

To paraphrase Winston Churchill, we are not at the beginning of the end but, rather, only at the end of the beginning of our intellectual and normative itinerary to master global governance as a tool for yesterday, today, and tomorrow. However, we should not be depressed with our slow progress in turning the global governance supertanker. It is crucial not to overlook previous steps, small and not so small, toward a more desirable world order. In short, we are not starting from scratch. Indeed, often it was not so much that the world changed as that observers noticed something that has long been there, or that they "rediscovered" something that was hardly new at all but had been overlooked. Of course, change has taken place. We should not underestimate the extent to which order, stability, and predictability exist despite the lack of a central authority to address the planet's woes. On any given day in virtually every corner of the world, exchanges take place smoothly, with neither notice nor comment. Mail is delivered among 200 countries. Travelers arrive at airports, harbors, train stations, and by road – many of them crossing borders with barely a notice. Goods and services move by land, air, sea, and cyberspace. A range of transboundary activities occur with the expectation of safety and security. In fact, disruptions and failures are often less frequent and spectacular in the international arena without an overarching central authority than within such countries as Afghanistan, Syria, Venezuela, and Zimbabwe that supposedly have functioning central governments.

That largely unseen economic, political, and technological structures enable the provision of some global public goods is uncontroversial. Moreover, there are perhaps more remarkable non-events: today there are no children dying from smallpox, and no nuclear weapon has been detonated in war since the two horrific explosions in Japan in 1945. While it is foolhardy to ignore widespread disease and poverty, it would also be myopic to ignore the progress that has resulted from human efforts to improve the lives and rights of citizens worldwide or the way that the world is governed.

While we have sought to emphasize that the human species is not starting from square one, nonetheless we would be ostrich-like and ahistorical to heave a sigh of relief and rest on our extremely limited laurels. The flourishing spectrum of international organizations, in fact, may contribute to concealing serious gaps in governance. If institutions exist that claim to govern specific domains but are not effective in so doing, they can shift public and diplomatic attention away from the genuine problems without actually solving them. A well-populated institutional terrain does not make an effective system of global governance. While today's system may be effective in many and often surprising ways, it would be hard to characterize it as anything except inadequate and unacceptable.

In short, cavernous gaps remain in the governance of today's world order. Alongside the positive stories of collaborative networks, there are demonstrations of the challenges that organizations share in moving toward the establishment of effective and institutionalized global governance. Without more solid foundations in international law and without more robust IGOs, today's mechanisms for better global governance are limited to voluntary participation, moral suasion, and peer pressure. These fledgling and inadequate contemporary structures of global governance must move beyond merely providing incentives for self-interested cooperation only when it suits or when it benefits elites for a handful of issues.

Governing the world at present reflects what Scott Barrett aptly labels "organized volunteerism."[1] But will global voluntary action alone suffice? Organizations routinely help ensure postal delivery and airline safety, to be sure, but too rarely address such grave problems as acid rain and ethnic cleansing. A new and appropriate global agenda would need to be far reaching, indeed.[2] Can the world be governed without institutions that have some supranational characteristics, starting with more robust versions of the current generation of IGOs, especially those with universal membership? Such a development would constitute what Coen and Pegram describe as the "third generation."[3]

The next step in our unfinished journey is to consider how we could think better about global governance and apply it normatively; how more humane global governance could result. We need to probe more deeply what has driven change and fostered continuity in different contexts – that is, what has triggered transformations versus encouraged modest adjustments and caused policies to endure. The understanding of global governance's complexity, time, space, and the everyday enables us to comprehend and parse distinctions between changes *of* global governance from more marginal changes *in* global governance so that we are able to advocate for more of the former that could make a genuine difference. Power, markets, technology, war (and its aversion), and ideas are examined as explanations for transitions in previous world orders and the bases for moving toward possible and more desirable future orders by accelerating desirable changes and mitigating undesirable inertia.

If we recuse ourselves from that journey, we may retain the dignity that George Orwell attributed to the condemned walking to the gallows after a storm in his retelling of "a hanging."[4] We may temporarily avoid treading in a puddle of rainwater on our way toward the noose. The outcome will, nonetheless, be the same.

Notes

Preface

1 Thomas G. Weiss and Rorden Wilkinson, "Rethinking Global Governance: Complexity, Authority, Power, Change," *International Studies Quarterly* 58/1 (2014): 207–15. This article was accompanied by critical commentary from Craig N. Murphy, "Global Governance over the Long Haul," *International Studies Quarterly* 58/1 (2014): 216–18; Mark Mazower, "Response," *International Studies Quarterly* 58/1 (2014): 219–20; and Martha Finnemore, "Dynamics of Global Governance: Building on What We Know," *International Studies Quarterly* 58/1 (2014): 221–4.

2 Thomas G. Weiss and Rorden Wilkinson, "Global Governance to the Rescue: Saving International Relations?" *Global Governance* 20/1 (2014): 19–36.

3 Thomas G. Weiss and Rorden Wilkinson, "Introduction" and "Change and Continuity in Global Governance," *Ethics & International Affairs* 29/4 (2015): 391–5 and 397–406; other contributors were Roland Paris, Catherine Weaver, Susan Park, and Craig N. Murphy, pp. 407–54.

4   Thomas G. Weiss and Rorden Wilkinson, "Global Governance beyond IR," in *International Relations Theory Today*, ed. Ken Booth and Toni Erskine (Cambridge: Polity, 2016), pp. 217–30.

5   Thomas G. Weiss and Rorden Wilkinson, "Continuity and Change in Global Governance," in *Rising Powers, Global Governance and Global Ethics*, ed. Jamie Gaskarth (London: Routledge, 2015), pp. 41–56.

6   Thomas G. Weiss and Rorden Wilkinson," The Globally Governed – Everyday Global Governance," *Global Governance* 24/2 (2018): 193–210.

7   Thomas G. Weiss and Rorden Wilkinson (eds), *International Organization and Global Governance* (2nd edn, London: Routledge, 2018).

8   See Alice Ba and Matthew J. Hoffmann (eds), *Contending Perspectives on Global Governance: Coherence, Contestation and World Order* (London: Routledge, 2005); and the contributions by Jason Charrette and Jennifer Sterling-Folker, "Realism," Christer Jönsson, "Classical Liberal Internationalism," Tana Johnson and Andrew Heiss, "Liberal Institutionalism," Duncan Snidal and Henning Tamm, "Rational Choice and Principal-Agent Theory," Susan Park, "Constructivism," Robert W. Cox, "Critical Theory," Julian Germann, "Marxism," Susanne Zwingel, Elisabeth Prügl, and Gülay Caglar, "Feminism," James Brassett, "Post-Structuralism," and Jacquelin Kataneksza, L. H. M. Ling, and Sara Shroff, "Decoloniality: (Re)Making Worlds," in *International Organization and Global Governance*, ed. Weiss and Wilkinson, pp. 91–218.

9   Klaus Dingworth and Philipp Pattberg, "Global Governance as a Perspective on World Politics," *Global Governance* 12/2 (2006): 187; and Weiss and Wilkinson, "Global Governance to the Rescue": 21–2.

10   Dingworth and Pattberg, "Global Governance": 188.

11   Lawrence Finkelstein, "What is Global Governance?" *Global Governance* 1/3 (1995): 367–8.

12   Michael Zürn, *A Theory of Global Governance: Authority,*

Legitimacy, and Contestation (Oxford: Oxford University Press, 2018).

13 See Rosemary Foot, John Lewis Gaddis, and Andrew Hurrell (eds), *Order and Justice in International Relations* (Oxford: Oxford University Press, 2003); and Laura Neack, *National, International and Human Security: A Comparative Introduction* (2nd edn, Lanham, MD: Rowman & Littlefield, 2017).

14 Craig N. Murphy, "Global Governance: Poorly Done and Poorly Understood," *International Affairs* 76/4 (2000): 789–804.

Introduction

1 Eric Arthur Blair, "Review of *The Good Earth*," *The Adelphi*, June 1931.

2 Synne L. Dyvik, Jan Selby, and Rorden Wilkinson (eds), *What's the Point of International Relations?* (London: Routledge, 2017).

3 Tim Dunne, Lene Hansen, and Colin Wight, "The End of International Relations Theory?" *European Journal of International Relations* 19/3 (2013): 405–25.

4 Richard Haass, *A World in Disarray: American Foreign Policy and the Crisis of the Old Order* (New York: Penguin, 2017).

5 George Orwell, "Politics and the English Language [1946]," in *Inside the Whale and Other Essays* (London: Penguin, 1962), pp. 143–57.

6 James N. Rosenau and Ernst Czempiel (eds), *Governance without Government: Order and Change in World Politics* (Cambridge: Cambridge University Press, 1992); David Goldblatt, Jonathan Perraton, David Held, and Anthony McGrew, *Global Transformations: Politics, Economics, Law* (Cambridge: Polity, 1999); Martin Hewson and Timothy J. Sinclair (eds), *Approaches to Global Governance Theory* (Albany: State University of New York Press, 1999); Alice Ba and Matthew J. Hoffmann (eds), *Contending Perspectives*

on *Global Governance: Coherence, Contestation and World Order* (London: Routledge, 2005); Ian Bache and Matthew V. Flinders (eds), *Multi-Level Governance* (Oxford: Oxford University Press, 2004); and David Held, *Global Covenant: The Social Democratic Alternative to the Washington Consensus* (Cambridge: Polity, 2004).

7 The Commission on Global Governance, *Our Global Neighbourhood* (Oxford: Oxford University Press, 1995).

8 Thomas G. Weiss (ed.), *Beyond UN Subcontracting: Task-Sharing with Regional Security Arrangements and Service-Providing NGOs* (Basingstoke: Macmillan, 1998); Steve Hughes and Rorden Wilkinson, "The Global Compact: Promoting Corporate Responsibility?" *Environmental Politics* 10/1 (2001): 155–9; and Sophie Harman, *Global Health Governance* (London: Routledge, 2011).

9 The following, while cited, are neither endorsed nor recommended reading: Pat Robertson, *The New World Order* (Dallas: World Publishing, 1992); Jim Keith, *Black Helicopters over America: Strikeforce for the New World Order* (Lilburn, GA: Illuminet Press, 1995); Dennis Laurence Cuddy, *Secret Records Revealed: The Men, the Money and the Methods behind the New World Order* (Oklahoma City: Hearthstone, 1999); and Jim Marrs, *Rule by Secrecy: The Hidden History that Connects the Trilateral Commission, the Freemasons, and the Great Pyramids* (New York: HarperCollins, 2001).

10 Paul F. Diehl (ed.), *The Politics of Global Governance: International Organizations in an Interdependent World* (5th edn, Boulder, CO: Lynne Rienner, 2005); and Margaret P. Karns, Karen A. Mingst, and Kendall W. Stiles, *International Organizations: The Politics and Processes of Global Governance* (3rd edn, Boulder, CO: Lynne Rienner, 2015).

11 Lorraine Elliott, "Global Environment Governance," in *Global Governance: Critical Perspectives*, ed. Rorden Wilkinson and Steve Hughes (London: Routledge, 2002), p. 57.

12 Our understanding of the long nineteenth and short twentieth centuries is drawn from Eric Hobsbawm's adaptation of

Fernand Braudel's notion of *"le long seizième siècle"* ("the long sixteenth century" of 1450-1640). See, Eric Hobsbawm, *The Age of Revolution: Europe 1789-1848* (London: Abacus Books, 1977); *The Age of Capital: 1848-1875* (London: Abacus Books, 1997); *The Age of Empire: 1875-1914* (London: Abacus Books, 1994); and *The Age of Extremes: The Short Twentieth Century, 1914-1991* (London: Abacus Books, 1995).

13 Craig N. Murphy, "The Last Two Centuries of Global Governance," *Global Governance* 21/2 (2015): 189.

14 Eric Helleiner, "Explaining the Globalization of Financial Markets: Bringing States Back In," *Review of International Political Economy* 2/2 (1995): 315-41; Rorden Wilkinson, "The WTO in Crisis: Exploring the Dimensions of Institutional Inertia," *Journal of World Trade* 35/3 (2001): 397-419; and Richard Woodward, *The Organisation for Economic Co-operation and Development* (London: Routledge, 2009).

15 Bruce D. Smith and Melinda A. Zeder, "The Onset of the Anthropocene," *Anthropocene* 4 (2013): 8-13.

16 Exceptions include Ellen Chesler and Terry McGovern (eds), *Women and Girls Rising: Progress and Resistance around the World* (London: Routledge, 2016); and Jim Yong Kim, Joyce V. Millen, Alec Irwin, and John Gershman (eds), *Dying for Growth: Global Inequality and the Health of the Poor* (Monroe, ME: Common Courage Press, 2000).

17 Gülay Caglar, Elisabeth Prügl and Susanne Zwingel (eds), *Feminist Strategies in International Governance* (London: Routledge, 2013).

18 Jamaica Kincaid, *A Small Place* (New York: Farrar, Straus, & Giroux, 2000).

19 George Orwell, "In Front of Your Nose," *Tribune*, 22 March 1946.

Chapter 1 The Global Governance Problématique

1 Fernand Braudel, *A History of Civilizations* (London: Penguin, 1995), p. 3.

2 See Bob Jessop, "Hollowing out the 'Nation-State' and Multilevel Governance," in *A Handbook of Comparative Social Policy*, ed. Patricia Kennett (2nd edn, Cheltenham: Edward Elgar, 2013), pp. 11-26.

3 For discussion, see John M. Hobson, *The State and International Relations* (Cambridge: Cambridge University Press, 2000).

4 See, most notably, Lawrence S. Finkelstein, "What Is Global Governance?" *Global Governance* 1/3 (1995): 367-72.

5 See, respectively, James N. Rosenau, "Governance in the Twenty-First Century," *Global Governance* 1/1 (1995): 13-43; and Klaus Dingwerth and Philipp Pattberg, "Global Governance as a Perspective on World Politics," *Global Governance* 12/2 (2006): 185-203.

6 David Held, "Elements of a Theory of Global Governance," *Philosophy and Social Criticism* 42/9 (2016): 837-46.

7 Martin Hewson and Timothy J. Sinclair, "Preface," in *Approaches to Global Governance Theory*, ed. Hewson and Sinclair (Albany: State University of New York Press, 1999), p. ix.

8 Charles Lindblom, "The Science of Muddling Through," *Public Administration Review* 19/2 (1959): 79-88.

9 Timothy J. Sinclair, *Global Governance* (Cambridge: Polity, 2012), p. 16.

10 Aseem Prakash and Jeffrey A. Hart (eds), *Globalization and Governance* (London: Routledge, 1999); David Held and Anthony McGrew (eds), *Governing Globalization* (Cambridge: Polity, 2002); and Robert W. Cox, "The Crisis of World Order and the Challenge to International Organization," *Cooperation and Conflict* 29/2 (1994): 99-113.

11 Richard B. Falk and Saul H. Mendlovitz (eds), *A Strategy of World Order*, 4 vols (New York: World Law Fund, 1966-7); and Grenville Clark and Louis B. Sohn, *World Peace through World Law* (Cambridge, MA: Harvard University Press, 1958).

12 Joseph Preston Barrata, *The Politics of World Federation*, 2 vols (Westport, CT: Praeger, 2004), vol. 2, pp. 534-5.

13 Michael Barnett and Raymond Duvall (eds), *Power in Global Governance* (Cambridge: Cambridge University Press, 2005), p. 1.

14 Michael Zürn, *A Theory of Global Governance: Authority, Legitimacy, and Contestation* (Oxford: Oxford University Press, 2018), p. 263.

15 Thomas G. Weiss and Ramesh Thakur, *The UN and Global Governance: An Unfinished Journey* (Bloomington: Indiana University Press, 2010).

16 Yoshikazu Sakamoto (ed.), *Global Transformations: Challenges to the State System* (Tokyo: United Nations University Press, 1992); Keith Krause and W. Andy Knight (eds), *State, Society and the UN System: Changing Perspectives on Multilateralism* (Tokyo: United Nations University Press, 1995); Robert W. Cox (ed.), *The New Realism: Perspectives on Multilateralism and World Order* (London: Macmillan, 1997); Stephen Gill (ed.), *Globalization, Democratization and Multilateralism* (London: Macmillan, 1997); Michael G. Schechter (ed.), *Future Multilateralism: The Political and Social Framework* (London: Macmillan, 1999) and *Innovation in Multilateralism* (London: Macmillan, 1999).

17 Robert W. Cox, "Introduction," in *The New Realism*, p. xvi.

18 John Gerard Ruggie (ed.), *Multilateralism Matters: The Theory and Praxis of an Institutional Form* (New York: Columbia University Press, 1993). Also Rorden Wilkinson, *Multilateralism and the World Trade Organisation: The Architecture and Extension of International Trade Regulation* (London: Routledge, 2000).

19 Edward Newman, Ramesh Thakur, and John Tirman (eds), *Multilateralism under Challenge? Power, International Order, and Structural Change* (Tokyo: United Nations University Press, 2006).

20 Nayan Chanda, "Runaway Globalization without Governance," *Global Governance* 14/2 (2008): 119-25.

21 Stuart Hall, "The Great Moving Nowhere Show," *Marxism Today* (November/December 1998): 11; and Eric Hobsbawm,

"The Death of Neo-Liberalism," *Marxism Today* (November/ December 1998): 5.

22 Robin Broad (ed.), *Global Backlash: Citizen Initiatives for a Just World Economy* (Lanham, MD: Rowman & Littlefield, 2002). See also Margaret E. Keck and Kathryn Sikkink, *Activists beyond Borders* (Ithaca, NY: Cornell University Press, 1998).

23 Rorden Wilkinson, *The WTO: Crisis and the Governance of Global Trade* (London: Routledge, 2006); Richard Peet, *Unholy Trinity: The IMF, World Bank and WTO* (London: Zed Books, 2003); and Louise Amoore (ed.), *The Global Resistance Reader* (London: Routledge, 2005).

24 UNDP, *Globalization with a Human Face: Human Development Report 1999* (New York: Oxford University Press, 1999). See also Diane Coyle, *Governing the Global Economy* (Cambridge: Polity, 2000); Raimo Väyrynen (ed.), *Globalization and Global Governance* (Lanham, MD: Rowman & Littlefield, 1999); David Held and Antony McGrew (eds), *Governing Globalization* (Cambridge: Polity, 2002); and Richard Falk, "Resisting 'Globalisation-from-above' through 'Globalisation-from-below,'" *New Political Economy* 2/1 (1997): 17–24.

25 Justin Rosenberg, "Escaping from the Prison of Political Science: What IR Offers That Other Disciplines Do Not," in *What's the Point of International Relations?*, ed. Synne L. Dyvik, Jan Selby, and Rorden Wilkinson (London: Routledge, 2017), pp. 219–30.

26 Harold K. Jacobson, *Networks of Interdependence: International Organizations and the Global Political System* (2nd edn, New York: Knopf, 1984), p. 84.

27 For example, Danilo Zolo, *Cosmopolis: Prospects for World Government* (Cambridge: Polity, 1997); and Luis Cabrera (ed.), *Global Governance, Global Government: Institutional Visions for an Evolving World System* (Albany: State University of New York Press, 2011). See also Thomas G. Weiss, "What Happened to the Idea of World Government?" *International Studies Quarterly* 53/2 (2009): 253–71.

28 Mark Mazower, *Governing the World: The History of an Idea* (New York: Penguin, 2012).

29 Craig N. Murphy, "Global Governance: Poorly Done and Poorly Understood," *International Affairs* 76/4 (2000): 789.

30 John Gerard Ruggie, *Constructing the World Polity* (London: Routledge, 1998), p. 2.

31 The label "emerging" should be treated critically. See Oliver Turner, "China's Recovery: Why the Writing Was Always on the Wall," *Political Quarterly* 80/1 (2009): 111-18. See also Christopher Layne, "The Unipolar Exit: Beyond the *Pax Americana*," *Cambridge Review of International Affairs* 24/2 (2011): 149-64. For what remains a pertinent counter, see Susan Strange, "The Persistent Myth of Lost Hegemony," *International Organization* 41/4 (1987): 551-74.

32 John Gerard Ruggie, "Third Try at World Order? America and Multilateralism after the Cold War," *Political Science Quarterly* 109/4 (1994): 553-70; and G. John Ikenberry, "A World Economy Restored: Expert Consensus and the Anglo-American Settlement," *International Organization* 46/1 (1992): 289-321.

33 Thomas Pogge, "Priorities of Global Justice," *Metaphilosophy* 32/1-2 (2001): 6-24; Peter M. Haas, "Epistemic Communities and International Policy Coordination," *International Organization* 46/1 (1992): 1-35; Diane Stone, "Governance via Knowledge: Actors, Institutions and Networks," in *Oxford Handbook of Governance*, ed. David Levi-Faur (Oxford: Oxford University Press, 2012), pp. 339-54; Eric Helleiner and Stefano Pagliari, "The End of an Era in International Financial Regulation? A Post-Crisis Research Agenda," *International Organization* 65/1 (2011): 169-200; and Philip G. Cerny, *Rethinking World Politics: A Theory of Transnational Neopluralism* (Oxford: Oxford University Press, 2010).

34 Louis Emmerij, Richard Jolly, and Thomas G. Weiss, *Ahead of the Curve? UN Ideas and Global Challenges* (Bloomington: Indiana University Press, 2001); Stephen Gill, "Constitutionalizing Inequality and the Clash of

Globalizations," *International Studies Review* 4/2 (2002): 47-65; and Martha Finnemore and Kathryn Sikkink, "International Norm Dynamics and Political Change," *International Organization* 52/4 (1998): 887–917.

35 Jeffrey Checkel, *Ideas and International Political Change: Soviet/Russian Behavior and the End of the Cold War* (New Haven, CT: Yale University Press, 1997).

36 Bruce W. Jentleson, "Global Governance in a Copernican World," *Global Governance* 18/2 (2012): 133–48.

37 Thomas Hale, David Held, and Kevin Young, *Gridlock* (Cambridge: Polity, 2013); Thomas Hale and David Held et al. (eds), *Beyond Gridlock* (Cambridge: Polity, 2017); and Rorden Wilkinson, "Gridlock? Maybe," *Philosophy and Public Issues* 6/3 (2016): 27–42.

38 Hendrik Spruyt, *The Sovereign State and its Competitors* (Princeton, NJ: Princeton University Press, 1994).

39 Eric Hobsbawm, *The Age of Empire: 1875-1914* (London: Abacus Books, 1994).

40 Hans J. Morgenthau, *Politics among Nations: The Struggle for Power and Peace* (6th edn, New York: McGraw-Hill, 1995), pp. 481-9.

41 Craig Murphy, *International Organization and Industrial Change: Global Governance since 1850* (Cambridge: Polity, 1994).

42 Christopher Chase-Dunn and Joan Sokolovsky, "Interstate Systems, World Empires and the Capitalist World Economy," *International Studies Quarterly* 27/3 (1983): 357–67.

43 André Gunder Frank and Barry K. Gills (eds), *The World System: Five Hundred Years or Five Thousand?* (London: Routledge, 2003).

44 John M. Hobson, *The Eastern Origins of Western Civilization* (Cambridge: Cambridge University Press, 2004).

45 Margaret Macmillan, *The Uses and Abuses of History* (New York: Random House, 2009).

46 E. H. Carr, *What is History?* (Harmondsworth: Penguin, 1961), p. 62.

47 Andrew J. Williams, Amelia Hadfield, and J. Simon Rofe, *International History and International Relations* (London: Routledge, 2012), p. 3.

48 Sinclair, *Global Governance*, p. 69.

49 Michael Barnett and Martha Finnemore (eds), *Rules for the World: International Organizations in Global Politics* (Ithaca, NY: Cornell University Press, 2004).

Chapter 2 Why History Matters

1 "Interview with H. G. Wells," *British Movietone*, BM6888, 17 August 1931.

2 For contemporary accounts, see G. T. Garratt, *Mussolini's Roman Empire* (Harmondsworth: Penguin, 1939); and F. Borkenau, *The New German Empire* (Harmondsworth: Penguin, 1939).

3 Craig N. Murphy, "The Last Two Centuries of Global Governance," *Global Governance* 21/2 (2015): 189; Amnon H. Eden, James H. Moor, J. H. Søraker, and Eric Steinhart (eds), *Singularity Hypotheses: A Scientific and Philosophical Assessment* (Berlin: Springer, 2012).

4 John M. Hobson, *The Eurocentric Conception of World Politics: Western International Relations Theory, 1760–2010* (Cambridge: Cambridge University Press, 2012).

5 Richard Phillips, *Mapping Men and Empire* (London: Routledge, 1997). For an overview of the uses (and abuses) of the term "*terra nullius*" as an instrument of dispossession, see Andrew Fitzmaurice, "The Genealogy of *Terra Nullius*," *Australian Historical Studies* 38/129 (2007): 1–15. On "*terra incognita*," see Carl Murray, "Mapping Terra Incognita," *Polar Record* 41/2 (2005): 103–12; and David Strang, "Contested Sovereignty: The Social Construction of Colonial Imperialism," in *State Sovereignty as Social Construct*, ed. Thomas J. Biersteker and Cynthia Weber (Cambridge: Cambridge University Press, 1996), pp. 31–4.

6 On borders, see, for example, Amitai Etzioni, "The Evils of Self-

Determination," *Foreign Policy* 89 (1992-3): 21-35; Roxanne Lynn Doty, *Imperial Encounters* (Minneapolis: University of Minnesota Press, 1996). On global trade governance, see Rorden Wilkinson, *What's Wrong with the WTO and How to Fix It* (Cambridge: Polity, 2014); and Erin Hannah, James Scott, and Silke Trommer (eds), *Expert Knowledge in Global Trade* (London: Routledge, 2015).

7   For two attempts otherwise, see Jim Yong Kim, Joyce V. Millen, Alec Irwin, and John Gershman (eds), *Dying for Growth: Global Inequality and the Health of the Poor* (Monroe, ME: Common Courage Press, 2000); and Jennifer Clapp and Rorden Wilkinson (eds), *Global Governance, Poverty and Inequality* (London: Routledge, 2010).

8   For insight, see Walter Scheidel (ed.), *Rome and China: Comparative Perspectives on Ancient World Empires* (Oxford: Oxford University Press, 2009).

9   Uma Kothari and Rorden Wilkinson, "Colonial Imaginaries and Postcolonial Transformations: Exiles, Bases, Beaches," *Third World Quarterly* 31/8 (2010): 1395-412.

10 See, for example, the discussion in Tim Marshall, *Divided: Why We're Living in an Age of Walls* (London: Elliott & Thompson, 2018).

11 Roy Moxham, "Salt Starvation in British India: Consequences of High Salt Taxation in Bengal Presidency, 1795 to 1878," *Economic and Political Weekly* 36/25 (2001): 2271-2; and Roy Moxham, *The Great Hedge of India* (London: Constable, 2002).

12 John Gerard Ruggie, "Multilateralism: The Anatomy of an Institution," *International Organization* 46/3 (1992): 566.

13 Ralph Fox, *The Colonial Policy of British Imperialism* (Oxford: Oxford University Press, [1933] 2008), p. 1.

14 Geoffrey M. Hodgson, *How Economics Forgot History: The Problem of Historical Specificity in Social Science* (London: Routledge, 2000); Paul A. David, "Path Dependence, its Critics and the Quest for 'Historical Economics,'" in *Evolution and Path Dependence in Economic Ideas*, ed. Pierre Garrouste

and Stavros Ioannides (Cheltenham: Edward Elgar, 2001), pp. 15-40; and Robert Chernomas and Ian Hudson, *Economics in the Twenty-First Century: A Critical Perspective* (Toronto: University of Toronto Press, 2016).

15 Andrew Hurrell, "Foreword to the Third Edition," in Hedley Bull, *The Anarchical Society* (3rd edn, New York: Columbia University Press, 2002), p. xiii.

16 Craig N. Murphy and JoAnne Yates, "The Globalizing Governance of International Communications: Market Creation and Voluntary Consensus Standard Setting," *Journal of Policy History* 27/3 (2015): 550-8; and Thomas G. Weiss and Rorden Wilkinson, "From International Organization to Global Governance," in *International Organization and Global Governance*, ed. Weiss and Wilkinson (2nd edn, London: Routledge, 2018), pp. 3-19.

17 Robert Jackson, *Sovereignty: The Evolution of an Idea* (Cambridge: Cambridge University Press, 2007), pp. 51-2.

18 Theda Skocpol, Peter B. Evans, and Dietrich Rüschemeyer (eds), *Bringing the State Back In* (New York: Cambridge University Press, 1985).

19 Susan Strange, *The Retreat of the State: The Diffusion of Power in the World Economy* (Cambridge: Cambridge University Press, 1996).

20 Tana Johnson, *Organizational Progeny: Why Governments Are Losing Control over the Proliferating Structures of Global Governance* (Oxford: Oxford University Press, 2014).

21 Robert Gerwarth, *The Vanquished: Why the First World War Failed to End, 1917-1923* (London: Penguin, 2017).

22 J. David Singer and Melvin Small, "The Composition and Status Ordering of the International System: 1815-1940," *World Politics* 18/2 (1966): 236-82; and Bruce M. Russet and W. Curtis Lamb, "Global Patterns of Diplomatic Exchange, 1963-1964," *Journal of Peace Research* 6/1 (1969): 37-55.

23 Inderjeet Parmar, *Foundations of the American Century: The Ford, Carnegie, and Rockefeller Foundations in the Rise of American Power* (New York: Columbia University Press, 2012).

24 James Scott and Rorden Wilkinson, "China Threat? Evidence from the WTO," *Journal of World Trade* 47/4 (2013): 761–82.

25 Francis Fukuyama, *The End of History and the Last Man* (New York: Free Press, 1992).

Chapter 3 Planetary Isn't the Point

1 J. M. Coetzee, *Waiting for the Barbarians* (London: Vintage Books, 2004), p. 169.

2 Robert W. Cox, "Introduction," in Cox (ed.), *The New Realism: Perspectives on Multilateralism and World Order* (London: Macmillan, 1997), p. xvi.

3 See, for example, Akira Iriye (ed.), *Global Interdependence: The World after 1945* (Cambridge, MA: Harvard University Press, 2014).

4 J. R. McNeill and William H. McNeill, *The Human Web: A Bird's-Eye View of World History* (New York: W. W. Norton, 2003).

5 Eric Hobsbawm, *The Age of Revolution, 1789–1848* (London: Abacus Books, 1995), p. 101.

6 See William Carr, *A History of Germany, 1815–1945* (London: St Martin's Press, 1969).

7 See Ian Tyrrell, *Transnational Nation: United States History in Global Perspective since 1789* (London: Palgrave Macmillan, 2015).

8 See David Olusoga, *The World's War: Forgotten Soldiers of Empire* (London: Head of Zeus, 2015); and Robert Gerwarth, *The Vanquished: Why the First World War Failed to End, 1917–1923* (London: Penguin, 2017).

9 Norman Stone, "Introduction," in H. G. Wells, *A Short History of the World* (London: Penguin, 1991), p. xiii.

10 Leland M. Goodrich, "From League of Nations to United Nations," *International Organization*, 1/1 (1947): 3–21.

11 M. Patrick Cottrell, *The League of Nations: Enduring Legacies of the First Experiment at World Organization* (New York: Routledge, 2018), pp. 45–6.

12 Robert W. Cox, "ILO: Limited Monarchy," in *The Anatomy of Influence: Decision Making in International Organization*, ed. Cox, Harold Jacobson, et al. (New Haven, CT: Yale University Press, 1973), p. 102; Robert W. Cox with Timothy Sinclair, *Approaches to World Order* (Cambridge: Cambridge University Press, 1996), p. 422; Stephen Hughes, "International Labour Standards: The Formation and Development of an International Regime – New Zealand and the International Labour Organisation, 1919-1945," unpubd PhD thesis, University of Auckland, 1999, pp. 38, 53.

13 E. H. Carr, *The Twenty Years' Crisis, 1919-1939* (2nd edn, London: Macmillan, 1991), pp. 27-31; John Maynard Keynes, *The Economic Consequences of the Peace* (London: Macmillan, 1920), p. 251; and Hans J. Morgenthau, *Politics among Nations: The Struggle for Power and Peace* (6th edn, New York: McGraw-Hill, 1985), pp. 94-500. See also A. G. MacDonnell, *England, their England* (London: Pan Books, 1933).

14 Morgenthau, *Politics among Nations*, p. 500.

15 Cottrell, *The League of Nations*, pp. 57-8.

16 Susan Pedersen, *The Guardians: The League of Nations and the Crisis of Empire* (Oxford: Oxford University Press, 2015).

17 Louis Emmerij, Richard Jolly, and Thomas G. Weiss, *Ahead of the Curve? UN Ideas and Global Challenges* (Bloomington: Indiana University Press, 2001).

18 M. Patrick Cottrell, "Lost in Transition? The League of Nations and the United Nations," in *Charter of the United Nations*, ed. Ian Shapiro and Joseph Lampert (New Haven, CT: Yale University Press, 2014), pp. 91-106.

19 Leland M. Goodrich, "From League of Nations to United Nations," *International Organization* 1/1 (1947): 3.

20 Franklin D. Roosevelt, "The Nations Have Common Objectives," speech given on 9 November 1943, www.ibiblio.org/pha/policy/1943/1943-11-09c.html.

21 Dan Plesch and Thomas G. Weiss (eds), *Wartime Origins and the Future United Nations* (London: Routledge, 2015).

22 Rorden Wilkinson, *What's Wrong with the WTO and How to Fix It* (Cambridge: Polity, 2014), pp. 183-7.
23 Frantz Fanon, *The Wretched of the Earth* (London: Penguin, 2001), p. 27.

Chapter 4 Global Governance in the Everyday

1 John K. Wright, "Terrae Incognitae: The Place of the Imagination in Geography," *Annals of the Association of American Geographers* 37/1 (1947): 1-15.
2 Exceptions are studies that tell us something about the receipt of global governance as an unexpected outcome of projects designed for other analytical purposes. For instance, Jim Yong Kim, Joyce V. Millen, Alec Irwin, and John Gershman (eds), *Dying for Growth: Global Inequality and the Health of the Poor* (Monroe, ME: Common Courage Press, 2000); and Ellen Chesler and Terry McGovern (eds), *Women and Girls Rising: Progress and Resistance around the World* (London: Routledge, 2016).
3 Caroline Nordstrom, *Global Outlaws: Crime, Money, and Power in the Contemporary World* (Berkeley: University of California Press, 2007).
4 Deborah D. Avant, Martha Finnemore, and Susan K. Sell (eds), *Who Governs the Globe?* (Cambridge: Cambridge University Press, 2010).
5 Michele Acuto, "Everyday International Relations: Garbage, Grand Designs and Mundane Matters," *International Political Sociology* 8/4 (2014): 345-62; John M. Hobson and Leonard Seabrooke (eds), *Everyday Politics of the World Economy* (Cambridge: Cambridge University Press, 2007); and Roger MacGinty, "Everyday Peace Bottom-Up and Local Agency in Conflict-Affected Societies," *Security Dialogue* 45/6 (2014): 548-64.
6 Anne-Marie Slaughter, "Everyday Global Governance," *Daedalus* 132/1 (2003): 83-90.
7 Thomas G. Weiss and Rorden Wilkinson, "From International

Organization to Global Governance," in *International Organization and Global Governance*, ed. Weiss and Wilkinson (2nd edn, London: Routledge, 2018), pp. 3–19; Craig N. Murphy and JoAnne Yates, "The Globalizing Governance of International Communications: Market Creation and Voluntary Consensus Standard Setting," *Journal of Policy History* 27/3 (2015): 550–8; and Maximilian Mayer and Michele Acuto, "The Global Governance of Large Technical Systems," *Millennium: Journal of International Studies* 43/2 (2015): 660–83.

8 Kirsten Gelsdorf, *Global Challenges and their Impact on International Humanitarian Action*, OCHA Occasional Policy Briefing Series, no. 1 (New York: UNOCHA, 2010).

9 Thomas G. Weiss, *Humanitarian Business* (Cambridge: Polity, 2013); and Alexander Betts, Louise Bloom, Josiah Kaplan, and Naohiko Omata, *Refugee Economies: Forced Displacement and Development* (New York: Oxford University Press, 2017).

10 Ian Talbot, 'The Punjab under Colonialism: Order and Transformation in British India," *Journal of Punjab Studies* 14/1 (2007): 3–10.

11 Rorden Wilkinson, "Changing Power Relations in the WTO: Why the India-U.S. Trade Agreement Should Make Us Worry More, Rather than Less, about Global Trade Governance," *Geoforum* 61 (2015): 13–16.

12 Yogesh Snehi, "Female Infanticide and Gender in Punjab: Imperial Claims and Contemporary Discourse," *Economic and Political Weekly* 38/41 (2003): 4302–5.

13 Ben Jacobs, "Donald Trump to Stick with NAFTA Free Trade Pact – for Now," *The Guardian*, 27 April 2017.

14 Katharine H. S. Moon, *Sex among Allies: Military Prostitution in U.S.-Korea Relations* (New York: Columbia University Press, 1997); and Cynthia Enloe, *Bananas, Beaches, and Bases: Making Feminist Sense of International Politics* (2nd edn, Berkeley: University of California Press, 2014).

15 Robert W. Cox (ed.), *The New Realism: Perspectives on Multilateralism and World Order* (London: Macmillan, 1997).

Chapter 5 Better and Better Global Governance

1 Scott Barrett, *Why Cooperate? The Incentive to Supply Global Public Goods* (Oxford: Oxford University Press, 2007), p. 19.
2 Diana Ayton-Shenker (ed.), *A New Global Agenda: Priorities, Practices, and Pathways of the International Community* (Lanham, MD: Rowman & Littlefield, 2018).
3 David Coen and Tom Pegram, "Wanted: A Third Generation of Global Governance Research," *Governance* 28/4 (2015): 417–20.
4 George Orwell, "A Hanging" [1931], in Orwell, *Decline of the English Murder and Other Essays* (London: Penguin, 1965), p. 16.

Index